BUY TO LET
PROPERTY STRATEGY

BY

MARK TEMPERLEY
MBA FCCA

Buy to Let Property Strategy
By Mark Temperley

1st. Edition 2007

ISBN 978-0-6151-4995-0

Exclusion of Liability and Disclaimer

While every effort has been made to ensure that this book provides accurate and expert guidance, it is impossible to predict all the circumstances in which it may be used. Accordingly, neither the author, publisher, retailer, nor any other suppliers shall be liable to any person or entity with respect to any loss or damage caused by the information contained in or omitted from this book. Investments and taxation are complex and this book is no substitute for professional advice.

This book is dedicated to my wife Dessislava,
who is my soulmate and my constant source of inspiration

Every man should listen to his wife, respect her sound advice,
because he needs a good woman to stop him doing silly things!

CHAPTERS

CHAPTER 1

INTRODUCTION

There are several books about how to be a landlord, detailing selecting property, selecting tenants, and tax.

This book is about making money, specifically about making money through investing in property over the long term. It does not offer any miracle cures or a quick get rich scheme but offers a strategy for making a good return on your investment over a period of time.

'IT'S SUCH A GOOD INVESTMENT'

Melanie Homes (**Daily Telegraph**: **26/08/2006**)

April and David Coulson, who live in Camberley in Surrey, are in the process of buying their first buy- to-let property and hope to rent it out later this year.

The couple are buying a two-bedroom flat in Bournemouth, Dorset, for £125,000 and see it as a long-term investment.

Mrs. Coulson, 38, who used to live in Bournemouth, said: "The flat needs a new kitchen, bathroom, carpets and re-decorating. We plan to rent it out for £750 a month and see it as a long-term retirement strategy. The rent won't cover all of the outgoings, so the flat will cost us between £50 and £100 a month to run."

Mr. and Mrs. Coulson chose to buy a property in Bournemouth because of its rental potential with young professional couples and because they can use it as a holiday home when it is not being rented out. "It's such a good investment. The main risk is if you can't afford the mortgage repayments."

A far far better headline to the sad story above would have been **"It's not a good investment at all".** The couple quoted in the Daily Telegraph are paying £600 and £1,200 per year so that somebody else can live in their property. Over 25 years they would pay between £15,000 and £30,000, on a property that will provide a return of £9,000 a year. I am making an assumption that the couple has a repayment mortgage where a part of the monthly payment repays the capital sum borrowed so that the end of the mortgage term there is no outstanding loan on the property. It will take two or three years *after they have paid off the mortgage* before the couple start to see any kind of profit – in 25 years time.

Use this book and make sure that you make money from a similar investment, from the first year onwards. Use this book to avoid mistakes such as the one above.

If the couple in the Daily Telegraph are buying the property in Bournemouth with an Interest Only mortgage the investment is even less advantageous. At the end of the mortgage term they will have paid between £15,000 and £30,000 and still have a mortgage to pay off on the property. It may be that prices will have risen and they will be able to sell the property for more than they paid with enough left over to cover what they have contributed and the capital gains tax on the profits. I sincerely hope that they have done their sums properly. There is a chapter at the end of the book which examines the possible results of their strategy as a case study.

"No man acquires property without acquiring with it a little arithmetic also"
Ralph Waldo Emerson

There are some calculations to do in this book. I have tried to minimise them to make the book more appealing but the fact remains that investing in property, along with making any other investments, is partly a mathematical exercise. The question that needs to be answered of course is "what return will I get for my investment?" or "would I be better off if I put my money in the building society?"

There are two key concepts to bear in mind throughout this book. The first of which is **profit**, the second of which is **cashflow**. The two are not the same at all and there is a section on the difference, which is important to understand, later in the book in Chapter 5.

There are some tax issues as well. Again, I have simplified these, because this is not a tax textbook. Tax does change and these changes do affect investment strategy. For example, until 2006 small companies with an annual profit of less than£10,000 paid no tax, which made them excellent ways of accumulating money tax free. Now the tax is 20%.

Where there are tax implications that affect decision making I have mentioned them and added a summary chapter. Tax calculations are based on current UK tax. Carl Bayley from Tax Cafe (www.taxcafe.co.uk) has written a good book explaining taxes on property and I recommend his book for those interested in the subject.

My belief is that to make money you have to work for it, and if some of the ideas proposed seem to involve work or effort, that is correct. If you do not do some work, such as running the numbers to see if the investment makes sense, or the preparatory footwork, you will have a lower chance of successful investing.

Good luck!

CHAPTER 2

WHY INVEST IN PROPERTY?

You can invest in many things – ISA's, unit trusts, investments companies, OIEC's, stocks and shares, bank deposit or savings accounts, insurance products…but investing in property has one key feature. **You can borrow to fund the investment**. Simply put, you can buy a £100,000 property with as little as £10,000. Not only this, somebody else will pay off the loan for you! No wonder property investment is so popular.

There are not many investments where you can do this. Yes, you can 'trade on the margin' if you buy stocks and shares, but if share prices go down the bank may call that margin and you have a cash call to fund. It's risky.

Yet, if the price of your property goes down the bank does not call and ask you for money. As the long as the original loan is being paid off each month there is no further demands for payment. The price of property can go up, and historically has done so quite dramatically. You can therefore obtain a god capital growth as well as receiving income.

No investment is without risk, and no doubt you've seen or heard the advertisement "you may not get back what you've paid" or "you home is at risk if you do not keep up payments secured on it". This year's headlines include "highest jobless for 5 years", "record UK debt levels", "bankruptcies soar" which are all pointers of a downturn in the economy.

This book shows you how to follow a route that enables you to make money over the long term even if property prices do fall. If you want to use property to supplement a pension this strategy in this book will work.

In order to obtain a loan you need to have the deposit and satisfy the lend institution that you can afford the repayments. Some lenders will only look at your salary or earnings; others take the rental income into account. A rule of thumb would be that the interest cover should be 130% of the monthly payments, so if the mortgage payment is £400 per month the rent needs to be £520.

It goes without saying that a good credit record is essential. You can get loan with a bad credit record but there are fewer lenders who are willing to provide a mortgage and the cost of borrowing (i.e. the interest rate) will usually be higher.

How to get and keep a good credit record

1. always make payments on time

2. check your credit score with a credit reference agency such as Experian

3. make sure you are not associated with other people at the same address

4. protect yourself from identity theft

5. do not have too many credit cards

6. do not make too many credit applications

7. make sure you are on the electoral roll at your application address

Key points from the chapter

- **Satisfying a lender that you can afford a mortgage is the key to property investments and you need to establish a good credit history**
- **Property investment is unique because it enables you to borrow money to fund the purchase. You do not need to put down the full purchase price.**
- **Somebody else (i.e. your tenants) will repay the loan for you.**

CHAPTER 3

STRATEGY

Why do you need a strategy?

In the Introduction I showed a couple who had a bad buy-to-let strategy. There are many people amongst the 767,000 buy -to-let investors in the UK, who have more than £89 million invested, who have jumped on the buy-to-let bandwagon with no real idea of what they are doing apart from reading about how great an investment it is in the popular press. And, as the paragraph in the introduction shows, do not rely on the press to give you good investment ideas!

You strategy is your target and setting your strategy decides on what kind of property investor you are going to be and what kind of property you are going to invest in. Deciding on one strategy does not prevent you from following another. If a good investment opportunity arises do not hesitate to seize it, whether in property or another investment.

As an investor you need to ask yourself some questions.

Fill out the boxes below.

Why are you interested in buying property? What is your goal?	
How long do you intend to keep the property for?	
Do you prefer houses or flats?	
Do you prefer new build or older property?	
Will you manage the property yourself or use	

an agent?	
How much time do you have available? How much do you want to be involved? Are you good at DIY?	
Where will you purchase property? How far from where you live?	
Are you numerate? Are you good at administration?	
How will you finance the purchase?	
What will you do in void periods (when the property is empty)	
Who is your target market?	
What is your attitude to risk?	
What return – in percentage terms -are you seeking on your investment?	

There are no 'right' answers but hopefully you have had to think about what you are doing and why you are doing it.

Implications of your answers

Question	Possible answers	Implications
Why are you interested in buying property? What is your goal?	To build up capital To supplement a pension in the future	You are in for the long term.
How long do you intend to keep the property for?	3 or 4 years	You are therefore interested in selling the property for a profit, which is fine if prices rise by more than the rate of interest on the mortgage. It also affects the type of property you will be interested in as you will loom for a property with capital appreciation.
	15+ years	You should follow the strategy in this book. You will need an older property with a steady income stream.. If you live in the South of England be prepared to travel to the North of England to find them.
Do you prefer houses or flats?	Flats.	**Read section below in chapter 16.**
Do you prefer new build or older property?	New build	There are a lot of new properties being built. Often they cost more than existing properties. Be aware that some lenders will no longer lend on new build flats due to the difficulty in valuing them as builders offer large discounts to purchasers.

Question	Possible answers	Implications
Will you manage the property yourself or use and agent?	Use an agent	Agent's fees can be expensive! As a minimum reckon on 10% plus VAT of 17.5% (11.75% in total) but some agents charge 12% of even 15%. The VAT brings the bill to 17.63% in the case of the last. However, a good agent can be good value as they will check tenants in and out, obtain references, collect the rent, deal with issues such as repairs. The agent's fees are tax deductible.
	Manage the property myself	Obviously there is a big cost saving but you need to consider how much work there is for you personally without an agent. You are the person who will get called at midnight because there is a water leak!
How much time do you have available? How much do you want to be involved? Are you good at DIY?	I work 9-5 so I don't have too much time available	You will need to use an agent. If you are not prepared to give up a weekend (or three) to clear up a property when a tenant moves out you need to use an agent. A month's empty property costs 8.3%. 6 weeks empty is 11.5% - roughly what an agent would cost so you might as well use the agent.
Where will you purchase property? How far from where you live?	Far	The further a property is away from where you live makes it harder for you personally to manage the property. It is essential that you use an agent. This affects the return on your investment.
	Near	You have the chance to manage the property if you want to.

16

Question	Possible answers	Implications
Are you numerate? Are you good at administration	Yes	You have the chance to save some money by preparing your own accounts and doing your own administration.
	No	You will need to use somebody to prepare your accounts and do your administration.
How will you finance the purchase?	Mortgage	You need to raise a minimum of 10% of the purchase price of the property plus some money for legal fees, survey, refurbishment, furnishings, etc.
	Cash	This generally means you pay 100% of the property price with nom borrowings. There are advantages to this when somebody wants to sell quickly and you can negotiate a lower than market price. Once you have bought the property you can then mortgage it.
What will you do in void periods (when the property is empty)		There are times when your property will be empty. This may be for redecoration, clearing out rubbish From exiting tenants for example. You will still need to pay the mortgage interest but have no rent coming in to cover it. Factor in at least 5%.
Who is your target market?	Working people	Good market but beware of couples who may split up.
	Professionals	Good market, but will expect modern well maintained properties

17

Question	Possible answers	Implications
	Students	Can offer a good return but there are sometimes problems. Always get a guarantor such as a parent (which also gives you an alternative address should you need to contact a student tenant later). Students do not generally treat property very well. However, they tend to move every year.
	Unemployed	Some lenders do not lend to landlords who target this market. My own experience is that these kind of tenants do not treat properties very well.
What is your attitude to risk?	I don't like risks at all	As a general rule taking higher risks is rewarded by higher returns. All investments carry some risk, and there is a risk with property.
What return – in percentage terms – are you seeking on your investment?	Less than 5%	You can obtain more than this by placing your money in a building society savings account
	Between 5% and 10%	This is a realistic expectation but you should aim for a higher return.
	Over 10%	You will have to work hard but returns of more than 10% are possible

There are several strategies for buy to let investors, although the most popular ones can be summarised as buy and sell and buy and hold. There are some variations of the first such as, such as buy, hold (renovate) and sell, or buy, live in and sell, but the key part of the strategy is to sell the property to realise a profit and receive cash.

The buy and sell strategy works well when prices are rising – property values have been known to double in some areas in the course of twelve months. However there are two factors to bear in mind. Firstly the profits are taxed, as much as 40% currently, unless you hold onto the property for several years when you receive a reduction in the amount of profit that is taxed. Secondly, the buy and sell strategy does not work well in a declining market.

Will property prices crash?

Let's examine the evidence in the short term, medium term and the long term.

Figure 1.1 – The Short Term

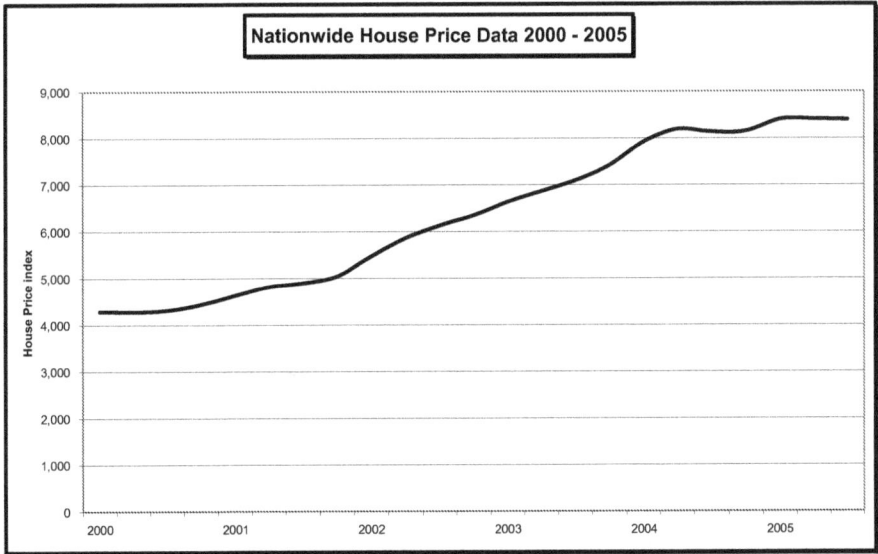

Nationwide House Price Data 2000 - 2005

Looking at the graph above the picture is rosy. In the short term, of 5 years, we can note that house prices have increased by some 104%, compared to an average inflation increase of 17%, average rise in wages of 17% and a stock market *decrease* of 16%. Indeed, it is this phenomenal rise that is attracting investors to the buy to let market. Just as the stock market can go down, so can the housing market, and you need a strategy to prepare for this probability.

I use the word *"probability"* rather than *"possibility"* because historical data over the medium term and longer term shows that house prices move in cycles.

A look at the medium term market, of 25 years, demonstrates that there is such a thing as house price deflation and a quick look at the graph of long term house prices shows why I believe that a crash may be coming.

Figure 1.2 – The Medium Term

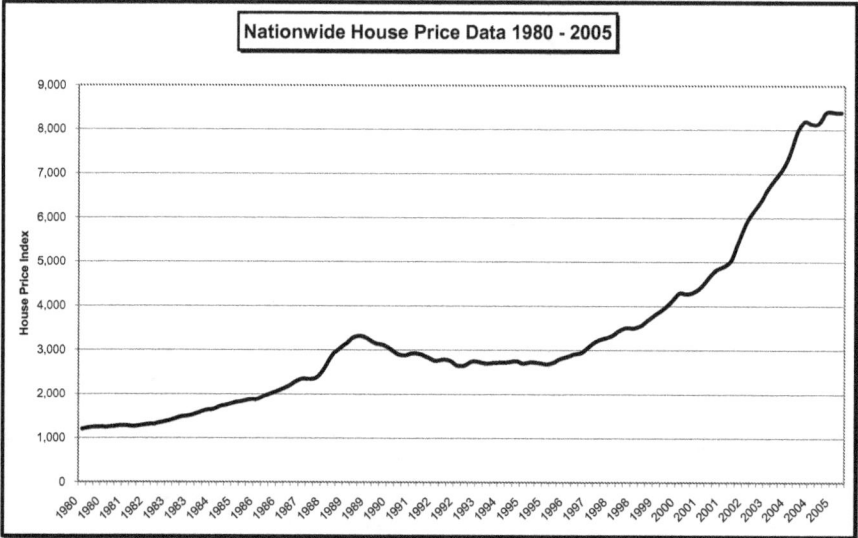

Nationwide House Price Data 1980 - 2005

As you can see, there are good reasons to believe the UK property market in 2006 is overvalued and may enter into a phase of decreasing prices. My personal estimate is that the market is overvalued by as much as 30%. Given that markets tend to overcorrect the prices could crash by as much as 50%. This may sound alarmist but prices certainly decreased by more than 30% in the early nineties. The Temperley Back to Back © strategy is designed to cope with holding property in any market situation.

Moreover, in mid-2006 the UK's unemployment rate has reached its highest point since October 2000 and the annual rise in joblessness, at 4.7 % in 2005, is the fastest since 1993. Interest rates have increased and are predicted to increase again and bankruptcies are increasing rapidly also. None of these give rise to an optimistic economic outlook. Furthermore, as first time buyers are priced out of the market it is akin to pulling the rug and a "correction" occurs. It may be that only the buy-to-let investor is preventing the crash by purchasing property that otherwise would be bought by first time buyers.

Figure 1.3 – The Long Term

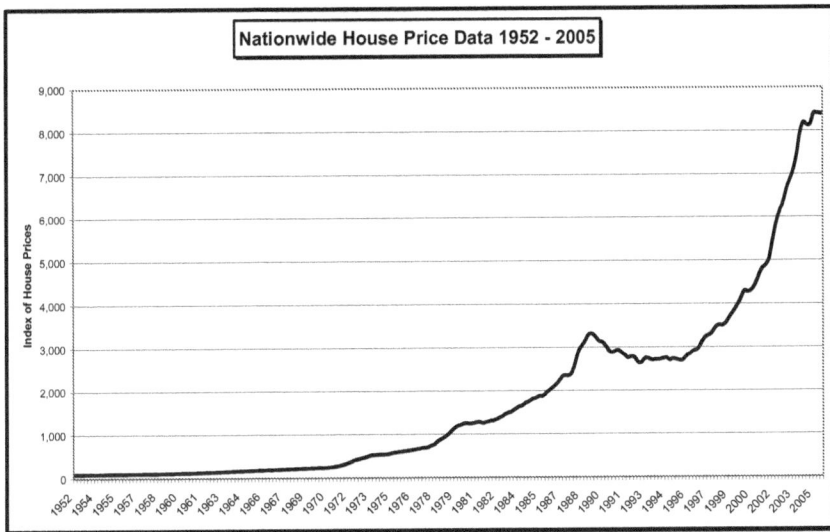

Nationwide House Price Data 1952 - 2005

You can see that house prices have risen dramatically over the long term and more importantly in the short term. When inflation is stripped out the effect is even more dramatic.

We see constant peaks and troughs and unless something unexpected happens it seems that we are overdue for a dip.

To cope with a declining market, or as an alternative strategy to one of the variations of buy and sell, if I have not convinced you that house prices may decrease at some future stage, there is a strategy of buy and hold, or buy and rent out. i.e. actually buy to let!

The other side of the coin

Whilst I personally believe that the UK property market is currently overpriced, it is worth pointing out that more than 600,000 people have immigrated to the UK since May 2004 when several East European nations joined the EU. The government was predicting that only 13,000 would come. Accordingly, planning for new homes fell short of what is required and with Bulgaria and Romania joining the EU in January 2007 the housing shortage will become worse. Given the low salary levels in these countries, the newcomers are not going to be in a position to buy, but will be renting for several years to come. And it is not just people from other countries who are finding it difficult to raise the money for a deposit on a house or flat. Non-immigrant youth also find it difficult and are living at home for longer or renting which gives a good rental market.

Buying and Letting Strategy (Buy and Hold)

This strategy works over the medium term, i.e. over 20 or 25 years. Thus, if you are aged 35 to 40 and intend to build up a property portfolio to fund or help fund a retirement pension, this strategy can work for you. This is not the same as investing in a SIPPS pension, but there are similarities.

The aims of the strategy are to produce a future income stream as a supplement to a pension. In fact we aim to better that as the income will be inflation protected and rise as incomes rise.

This strategy is therefore about producing long term income cashflows by holding a property portfolio and not short terms capital gains by buying and selling property.

Key points from the chapter

- **If you don't know where you are going, any road will take you there. Therefore you need a strategy to guide you.**
- **Property prices may fall, but this will not concern you. They may rise due to an increase in demand. The rise may concern you because you need to invest more due to higher prices, but of more importance is the demand for rented accommodation.**
- **You should make a long term investment.**

CHAPTER 4

TYPES OF MORTGAGES

The classic strategy for buying property is to borrow money as a mortgage secured on the property. This typically involves borrowing money over a period of 20 or 25 years, with you, the investor, making an initial investment of between 10 and 25% of the property value.

There are two principle types of mortgages – interest only and repayment.

Interest Only Mortgage

Many buy to let investors take out a simple repayment mortgage. However, in the long term you still have to repay the capital, or sell the property. As we have seen in the previous chapter, there is no guarantee that property prices will continue to rise and a strategy of using only interest only mortgages is therefore risky.

In a repayment mortgage the payments are higher as part of the monthly payment repays a part of the capital amount borrowed. There are some tax advantages too in taking out an interest only mortgage as you still obtain an interest deduction but the amount is less, particularly towards the end of the mortgage term. The reason for having an interest only mortgage is shown on the chart below.

Capital and Interest Repayments over 25 years

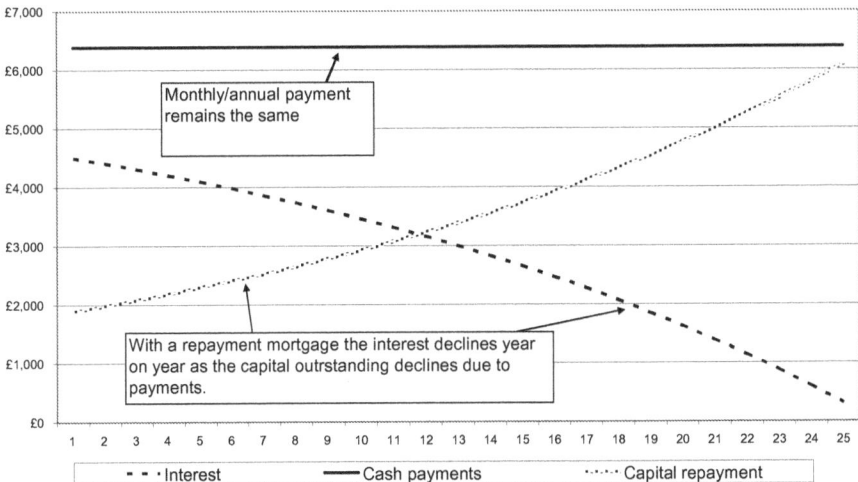

Monthly/annual payment remains the same

With a repayment mortgage the interest declines year on year as the capital outrstanding declines due to payments.

- - · Interest   ——— Cash payments   ······ Capital repayment

With an interest only mortgage you pay less tax as the amount of interest that can be deducted from your tax bill remains the same each year. You have the problem of how to repay the mortgage at the end of the term without selling the property.

Repayment Mortgage

With a repayment mortgage, over a period of time the amount of payment you make each month is the same. However, the payment includes an element of capital repayment and the amount of capital outstanding decreases over time. As the outstanding capital amount decreases, so does the interest. The consequence of this is that there is less and less tax relief each year on the mortgage payments, which means you pay more tax on the profits each year.

Nevertheless, having a repayment mortgage is an attractive option if cashflow permits, because at the end of the mortgage period you own a property with no outstanding loan. In other words, at the end of the mortgage period, the rental income is the profit (except for small charges such as insurance).

Example of differences between interest only mortgage and repayment mortgage

Amount of mortgage	**£100,000**
Interest Rate	**5%**
Interest only Mortgage	
Annual Interest Payment	£5,000
Monthly Interest Payment	£417
Repayment Mortgage	
Annual repayment of interest and capital (over 25 years)	£7,015
Monthly repayment of interest and capital	£585

The repayment mortgage costs, in cashflow terms, a lot more than a simple interest only mortgage.

Let's next examine strategies based on both types of mortgages.

Key points from the chapter

- **House prices can go up and down over a period of time. However, predictions about the direction of future prices are often inaccurate. You need a strategy that works irrespective of what happens to prices.**

- **Repayment mortgages cost significantly more in terms of cash repayments than interest only mortgages but are the desirable option for the long run because at the end of the mortgage term you own the property outright.**

CHAPTER 5

CALCULATING WHETHER TO INVEST IN A PROPERTY AS A BUY TO LET INVESTMENT

In this chapter we look at how you calculate whether it is worth investing in a property or not. In Chapter 3 you answered the question on how much you expected as a return on your investment. In my view do not accept less than 5% more than you can obtain on a bank or building society deposit. As you can receive 5% today from a bank deposit account or building society savings account, you should not accept less than 10%. This compensates for the work you have to do, as well as the risk (of void periods, bad tenants). The exception to this is where prices are increasing rapidly and your strategy is not to hold a property for the long term but to sell in the short term,

Let's use the following figures:

Purchase Price of Property	£100,000
Deposit %	10%
Deposit £	£10,000
Legal fees	£400
Survey	£400
Stamp duty	Nil
Mortgage arrangement fee	£199
Refurbishment	Nil
Furniture	Nil
Rental Income per month	£550
Rental Income per year	£6,600
Agents Fees	£776
Insurance	£100
Repairs	£200
Rate of interest	5%
Mortgage Interest	£333

Using the figures above you can calculate the profit or loss on the property.

Rental Income	6,600
Expenses	5,576
Profit	**1,025**

Profit is £1,025 per year which gives a return of 9.3%

(Profit of £1,025 / Investment of £10,999 x 100)

Tax is 40% (£410) so the after tax profit is £615.

Calculate what the return is on the properties in the examples below:

Example 1

There is a house for sale at £100,000. You can raise 10% of the asking price as a deposit, legal fees are £300, survey costs are £300, but there are refurbishment costs of £2,000 and afterwards furnishing costs of £1,500.

The house will rent for £600 per month when it has been refurbished and furnished. The mortgage interest rate is 5%, there is an agent's fee of 10% plus VAT of 17.5%, buildings insurance is £100, and you can expect repairs of £200 over a 12 month period.

Example 2

There is a house for sale at £150,000. You can raise 10% of the asking price as a deposit, legal fees are £300, survey costs are £300, but there are refurbishment costs of £2,000 and afterwards furnishing costs of £1,500.

The house will rent for £750 per month when it has been refurbished and furnished. The mortgage interest rate is 5%, there is an agent's fee of 10% plus VAT of 17.5%, buildings insurance is £100, and you can expect repairs of £200 over a 12 month period.

Example 3

There is a flat for sale at £45,000. You can raise 10% of the asking price as a deposit, legal fees are £300, survey costs are £300, but there are refurbishment costs of £2,000 and afterwards furnishing costs of £1,500.

The house will rent for £250 per month when it has been refurbished and furnished. The mortgage interest rate is 5%, there is an agent's fee of 10% plus VAT of 17.5%, buildings insurance is £100, **a service charge of £200 per year** and you can expect repairs of £200 over a 12 month period.

Example 4

There is a flat for sale at £130,000. You can raise 10% of the asking price as a deposit, legal fees are £300, survey costs are £300, but there are refurbishment costs of £2,000 and afterwards furnishing costs of £1,500.

The house will rent for £250 per month when it has been refurbished and furnished. The mortgage interest rate is 5%, there is an agent's fee of 10% plus VAT of 17.5%, buildings insurance is £100, **a service charge of £200 per year** and you can expect repairs of £200 over a 12 month period.

Compare your calculations with the answers below.

Example 1
Property Price   100,000

Deposit	10%	10,000
Legal fees		300
Survey fees		300
Refurbishment		2,000
Furniture		1,500
Total Investment		**14,100**

Mortgage amount   90,000
Rent per month   600

Annual Rental	7,200
Mortgage interest @ 5%	-4,500
Insurance	-100
Repairs	-200
Agent fee	-846
Annual profit	**1,554**

Return on investment (before tax)	**11%**

Example 2

Property Price		150,000

Deposit	10%	15,000
Legal fees		300
Survey fees		300
Refurbishment		2,000
Furniture		1,500
Total Investment		**19,100**

Mortgage amount		135,000
Rent per month	750	

Annual Rental	9,000
Mortgage interest @ 5%	-6,750
Insurance	-100
Repairs	-200
Agent fee	-1,058
Service charge	
Annual profit	**893**

Return on investment (before tax)	**5%**

Example 3

Property Price		45,000

Deposit	10%	4,500
Legal fees		300
Survey fees		300
Refurbishment		2,000
Furniture		1,500
Total Investment		**8,600**

Mortgage amount		40,500
Rent per month	250	

Annual Rental	3,000
Mortgage interest @ 5%	-2,025
Insurance	-100
Repairs	-200
Agent fee	-353
Service charge	-200
Annual profit	**123**

Return on investment (before tax)	**1%**

Example 4

Property Price		130,000

Deposit	10%	13,000
Legal fees		300
Survey fees		300
Refurbishment		2,000
Furniture		1,500
Total Investment		**17,100**

Mortgage amount		117,000
Rent per month	550	

Annual Rental	6,600
Mortgage interest @ 5%	-5,850
Insurance	-100
Repairs	-200
Agent fee	-776
Service charge	-200
Annual profit	**-526**

Return on investment (before tax)	**-3%**

For every property you consider buying, you **must** make a similar calculation. If the return does not meet your minimum return, walk away. There are quite literally millions of properties to choose from.

Note:

You can of course adapt this formula for your own needs. You might, for example, add in a void period, or other known regular expenses such as accountancy fees or travel and telephone costs.

It is important that you make a calculation for each property you are thinking of buying. Also important is to understand the concept of cashflow as well as the concept of profit.

Cashflow versus Profit

As mentioned in the introduction these two key concepts are not the same. They are related, but different. It is possible to make a profit but incur a negative cashflow. The ideal is to make a profit and generate a positive cashflow.

If profit is your revenue less expenses why is the cashflow different? The answer is because of the tax treatment of certain activities and the type of mortgage selected.

In some circumstances there is a wear and tear allowance of 10% of rental income. As soon as you see the word "allowance" you know that there will be a difference between what you actually pay in cash and what your allowance is. It is similar to being given a meal allowance of £30 on a business trip but only spending £25. You will have a difference of £5. In the case of the wear and tear allowance you can claim the allowance as a tax deduction and reduce the tax paid, but in cash terms you have not paid out the allowance.

The main difference occurs when you choose a repayment mortgage. Only the interest part is deducted from the revenue to arrive at a profit. As mentioned before, a repayment mortgage includes in the monthly repayment an element of the sum borrowed.

Example 1

Rental income is £500 per month, or £6,000 per year. Interest payments are £4,000 per year. As the property is rented out furnished you can claim a 10% wear and tear allowance.

We need to calculate the profit first before the cashflow. The profit is the income of £6,000 less £4,000 of interest and less £600 of wear and tear allowance. This gives a taxable profit of £1,400 and the tax at 40% is £560. Profit after tax is therefore £840.

The cashflow however is different. It is the £6,000 of income less £4,560 of expenses to give a positive cashflow of £1,440. The difference between the two figures is the wear and tear allowance and the tax.

The complications come when choosing types of mortgages. In the above example we assumed an interest only mortgage. The amount paid each month is higher than an interest only mortgage because it includes a repayment of the amount borrowed.

Example 2

Using the example above but with a repayment mortgage of £6,500 per year.

Again, we must start with the profit, which is exactly the same. The extra payments for the mortgage do not affect the profit.

However, the cashflow is different. This is £6,000 of income less £7,060 of expenses to give a negative cashflow of £1,060.

This is the similar to the Daily Telegraph example mentioned in the Introduction. Of course, the repayments can be lower than the income and generate a positive cashflow but at the current level of property prices this is unlikely.

When calculating whether to invest in a property you need to make two calculations. The first is the return on the investment, the second is the cash generated. There is no point in investing in a property if you end up having to make a contribution to the mortgage each month. When getting a quote for a mortgage make sure you get the amount of monthly payment for both the interest only mortgage and the repayment mortgage.

Key points from the chapter

- **Calculate the return on a potential property to see if it is worth investing in. Does the return meet your minimum acceptable return?** I suggest going to the Rightmove website (www.rightmove.co.uk) and selecting a town with which you are unfamiliar and seeing what property is selling for, and what it rents out for, to calculate the potential returns.

- **There is an important difference between cashflow and profit and it is important that you understand this.**

CHAPTER 6

BUY TO LET STRATEGIES

Strategy A – Interest Only Mortgage

This strategy is for an investor to borrow money using an interest only mortgage, and sell the property at some time in the future as prices rise. In the meantime there is enjoyment of an income from the property. However, note that at some point the property must be sold to repay the mortgage. This may be in 20, 25 or 30 years time, but after this there is no income stream once the property has been sold. There is an assumption that any money left over once tax has been paid is invested in an interest bearing account.

Using the following simplified assumptions, we can see the effects of selecting each type of mortgage. (I have omitted legal costs, tax, repairs – this example is just for illustrative purposes to compare the strategies)

Purchase price of property	£100,000
Mortgage	£90,000
Mortgage Interest Rate	5%
Monthly Rental	£500

The annual cashflow is rental income of £6,000 less mortgage interest of £4,500 leaving £1,500 per year of profit. It would take 60 years to generate enough cash to repay the mortgage, and this is before you have paid any tax on the profit. You might get lucky and find property prices increase and you make money by selling the property in the future, although as we have seen, prices have gone down dramatically in the past and may well do so in the future.

Another option is to buy several properties, and use the excess cashflow to repay the mortgage. You would need several of them to generate enough cash to repay the mortgage, and the catch is that lenders often limit you to a maximum of ten properties.

This equates to needing 4 properties to end up with a single one at the end.

Strategy B – Repayment mortgage

In the ideal world we know that the rental income exceeds the mortgage payments; indeed, many lenders require that the rent is 125% of the mortgage payment. However, a repayment mortgage is much more expensive.

For example, on a £100,000 property with a mortgage of £80,000 at an interest rate of 5%, the monthly payments on an interest only mortgage are £333. This indicates a minimum rent of £417 is needed to satisfy lenders' requirements. But, on a repayment mortgage the monthly repayments are £466 on a 25 year loan and £528 on a 20 year loan.

In many cases the amount of rental income received would not cover the mortgage payments in the case of a repayment mortgage.

Using the data from Strategy A we find that in terms of cashflow we have a rental income of £500 per month and mortgage interest repayments of £526 per month, or £26 per month (£312 per year) less rent than the mortgage payments. In other words, using the highly desirable repayment mortgage leads to a cash outflow, whereas as investors (as opposed to Daily Telegraph readers) we want a cash inflow.

How can we solve this dilemma?

CHAPTER 7

INTRODUCING TEMPERLEY'S BACK TO BACK© MODEL

Strategy C – use Temperley's Back to Back© Model

The answer is to buy two properties, one with an interest only mortgage, the second with a repayment mortgage. I have termed this as **"Back to Back"**.

Temperley's Back to Back© Model combines the advantages of both these type of mortgages to produce a winning strategy of succeeding in buy to let investment over the medium term and even if house prices fall

Firstly a property is purchased with an interest only mortgage. The second property is purchased with a repayment mortgage. **This equates to needing just 2 properties to end up with 1 at the end.**

It is very important that the properties are purchased in that order for the strategy to work (unless you purchase 2 properties at the same time)

Combining the two examples above you would have the following:

Income/ Expense	Property 1	Property 2	Combined
	Interest Only	Repayment	
Revenue	£6,000	£6,000	£12,000
Mortgage payments	£5,000	£6,312	£11,312
Net	£1,000	-£312	£688

Combining the two types of mortgage enable you to buy a property with a repayment mortgage that in the long term you will own without a mortgage. This is of course before the taxation of any profits.

Let us now look at a more complicated example to see how the model could be used.

Full model assumptions

Purchase Price of Property	£100,000
Deposit %	10%
Deposit £	£10,000
Legal fees	£400
Survey	£300
Stamp duty	Nil
Mortgage arrangement fee	£199
Refurbishment	Nil
Furniture	Nil
Rental Income per month	£600
Rental Income per year	£7,200
Agents Fees	£846
Insurance	£80
Repairs	£150
Rate of interest	5.0%
Mortgage Interest	£4,500
Interest on deposit accounts	5%
Personal tax rate	40%

This gives a cash inflow from an interest only mortgage of £1,208 per year and a cash outflow of £608 (in the first year) for the repayment mortgage. The amount of cash for a repayment mortgage changes each year because although the repayments are the same each month, the amount of capital is decreasing all the time. Consequently the amount of interest is changing. As the interest decreases as the capital is paid off and therefore reduced, the profit increases and tax increases.

Let's have a look at combining the cashflows using the Back to Back© Model.

	PAIR 1			
	1st. House	2nd. House	Net Interest	Cumulative CF
Year 1	1,208	-608	0	599
Year 2	1,208	-646	18	1,179
Year 3	1,208	-686	35	1,737
Year 4	1,208	-727	52	2,269
Year 5	1,208	-771	68	2,774
Year 6	1,208	-816	83	3,249
Year 7	1,208	-864	97	3,690
Year 8	1,208	-915	111	4,093
Year 9	1,208	-968	123	4,456
Year 10	1,208	-1,024	134	4,774
Year 11	1,208	-1,082	143	5,043
Year 12	1,208	-1,143	151	5,259
Year 13	1,208	-1,208	158	5,417
Year 14	1,208	-1,275	163	5,512
Year 15	1,208	-1,346	165	5,539
Year 16	1,208	-1,421	166	5,492
Year 17	1,208	-1,499	165	5,366
Year 18	1,208	-1,581	161	5,154
Year 19	1,208	-1,667	155	4,849
Year 20	1,208	-1,758	145	4,444
Year 21	1,208	-1,853	133	3,932
Year 22	1,208	-1,953	118	3,305
Year 23	1,208	-2,058	99	2,554
Year 24	1,208	-2,168	77	1,671
Year 25	1,208	-2,283	50	645
Year 26	1,208	4,509	19	6,381
Year 27	1,208	4,509	191	12,290
Year 28	1,208	4,509	369	18,375
Year 29	1,208	4,509	551	24,643
Year 30	1,208	4,509	739	31,100

Cashflow of Pair with interest only and repayment mortgages

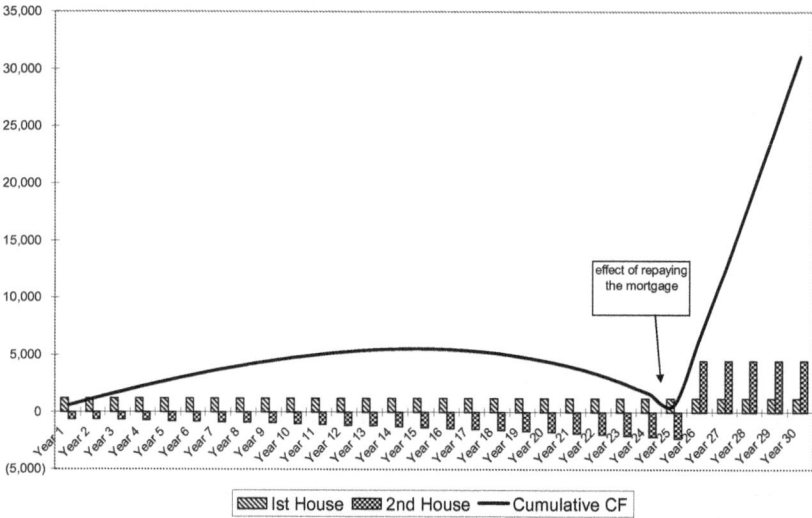

The cashflow really takes off once the repayment mortgage is paid off. Suddenly all the expense of the mortgage repayments are released and the increase in cashflow accumulates dramatically. The interest only mortgage subsidises the repayment mortgage and enables you to own a property outright at the end of the mortgage period.

The Back to Back© Model takes this pairing technique as a base and expands it to further pairs. Each pair is self subsidizing and enables the eventual ownership of a property.

	PAIR 1 + PAIR 2		
	1ST PAIR	2ND PAIR	CUMULATIVE
YEAR 1	599		599
YEAR 2	580	599	1,778
YEAR 3	558	580	2,915
YEAR 4	533	558	4,006
YEAR 5	505	533	5,044
YEAR 6	475	505	6,023
YEAR 7	441	475	6,939

	PAIR 1 + PAIR 2		
	1ST PAIR	2ND PAIR	CUMULATIVE
YEAR 8	404	441	7,783
YEAR 9	363	404	8,549
YEAR 10	318	363	9,230
YEAR 11	269	318	9,817
YEAR 12	216	269	10,302
YEAR 13	158	216	10,676
YEAR 14	95	158	10,929
YEAR 15	27	95	11,051
YEAR 16	-47	27	11,032
YEAR 17	-126	-47	10,858
YEAR 18	-212	-126	10,520
YEAR 19	-305	-212	10,003
YEAR 20	-405	-305	9,293
YEAR 21	-512	-405	8,376
YEAR 22	-627	-512	7,237
YEAR 23	-751	-627	5,859
YEAR 24	-883	-751	4,225
YEAR 25	-1,026	-883	2,316
YEAR 26	5,736	-1,026	7,027
YEAR 27	5,908	5,736	18,671
YEAR 28	6,086	5,908	30,665
YEAR 29	6,268	6,086	43,019
YEAR 30	6,456	6,268	55,743

	PAIR 1 + PAIR 2 + PAIR 3			
	1ST PAIR	2ND PAIR	3RD PAIR	CUMULATIVE
YEAR 1	599			599
YEAR 2	580	599		1,778
YEAR 3	558	580	599	3,515
YEAR 4	533	558	580	5,185
YEAR 5	505	533	558	6,780
YEAR 6	475	505	533	8,293
YEAR 7	441	475	505	9,713
YEAR 8	404	441	475	11,032
YEAR 9	363	404	441	12,239
YEAR 10	318	363	404	13,323
YEAR 11	269	318	363	14,273
YEAR 12	216	269	318	15,076
YEAR 13	158	216	269	15,719

YEAR 14	95	158	216	16,188
YEAR 15	27	95	158	16,468
YEAR 16	-47	27	95	16,544
YEAR 17	-126	-47	27	16,398
YEAR 18	-212	-126	-47	16,012
YEAR 19	-305	-212	-126	15,369
YEAR 20	-405	-305	-212	14,447
YEAR 21	-512	-405	-305	13,225
YEAR 22	-627	-512	-405	11,681
YEAR 23	-751	-627	-512	9,792
YEAR 24	-883	-751	-627	7,530
YEAR 25	-1,026	-883	-751	4,870
YEAR 26	5,736	-1,026	-883	8,697
YEAR 27	5,908	5,736	-1,026	19,316
YEAR 28	6,086	5,908	5,736	37,046
YEAR 29	6,268	6,086	5,908	55,308
YEAR 30	6,456	6,268	6,086	74,118

PAIR 1 + PAIR 2 + PAIR 3 + PAIR 4				
	1ST PAIR	2ND PAIR	3RD PAIR		CUMULATIVE
YEAR 1	599				599
YEAR 2	580	599			1,778
YEAR 3	558	580	599		3,515
YEAR 4	533	558	580	599	5,784
YEAR 5	505	533	558	580	7,959
YEAR 6	475	505	533	558	10,029
YEAR 7	441	475	505	533	11,982
YEAR 8	404	441	475	505	13,807
YEAR 9	363	404	441	475	15,488
YEAR 10	318	363	404	441	17,013
YEAR 11	269	318	363	404	18,366
YEAR 12	216	269	318	363	19,532
YEAR 13	158	216	269	318	20,493
YEAR 14	95	158	216	269	21,231
YEAR 15	27	95	158	216	21,727
YEAR 16	-47	27	95	158	21,961
YEAR 17	-126	-47	27	95	21,910
YEAR 18	-212	-126	-47	27	21,551
YEAR 19	-305	-212	-126	-47	20,861
YEAR 20	-405	-305	-212	-126	19,813

PAIR 1 + PAIR 2 + PAIR 3 + PAIR 4				
	1ST PAIR	2ND PAIR	3RD PAIR		CUMULATIVE
YEAR 21	-512	-405	-305	-212	18,379
YEAR 22	-627	-512	-405	-305	16,530
YEAR 23	-751	-627	-512	-405	14,236
YEAR 24	-883	-751	-627	-512	11,462
YEAR 25	-1,026	-883	-751	-627	8,175
YEAR 26	5,736	-1,026	-883	-751	11,252
YEAR 27	5,908	5,736	-1,026	-883	20,987
YEAR 28	6,086	5,908	5,736	-1,026	37,692
YEAR 29	6,268	6,086	5,908	5,736	61,690
YEAR 30	6,456	6,268	6,086	5,908	86,408

As you can see from the figures above, you accumulate quite a lot of capital with 3 or more properties. So much so, that you will be able to repay one of the interest only mortgages in addition to the repayment mortgages. Additionally, when inflation has been taken into consideration, there are is scope for enough capital to be accumulated to purchase one, perhaps two, additional interest only properties. The inflation effect is dealt with in a later chapter.

Effect of adding more pairs

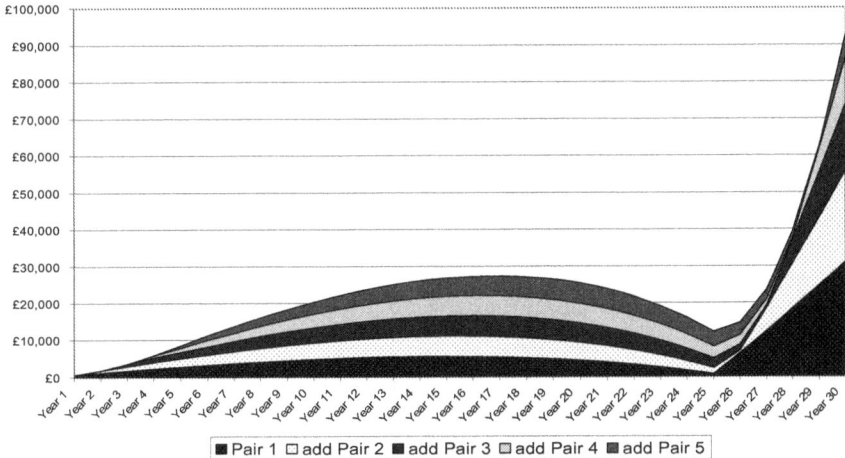

Pair 1 □ add Pair 2 ■ add Pair 3 □ add Pair 4 ■ add Pair 5

The **Temperley Back to Back© Model,** using 3 pairs of properties, enables a long term investor to:

- Purchase 3 properties with repayment mortgages
- Build up a capital sum to purchase at least one of the other three remaining properties, perhaps two or even three depending on inflation.

At the end of the 25 or 30 year period you will own at least 4 properties outright, which if rented out for £600 per month will give an income of £28,000 (less some expenses). This is a useful supplement to any pension, and has the added advantage that rents should keep pace with inflation.

Attractive as the model is, there are some people who cannot purchase two properties every year, or for whom the idea of having a negative cashflow (before the interest converts it back to a positive cashflow) is not appealing. In this case the **Back to Back© Model** can be adapted. The same basic principle applies – first you **must** purchase a property with an interest only mortgage. This allows you to build up some cash reserve which you will need to subsidise the cash outflows on the repayment mortgage. At a later date (the model assumes the same year and I assume with a year's delay, but this could be a longer period) the second property is purchased with a repayment mortgage.

	PAIR 1 with 1 year delay			
	Ist House	2nd House	Net Interest	Cumulative CF
Year 1	1,208			1,208
Year 2	1,208	-608	36	1,843
Year 3	1,208	-646	55	2,460
Year 4	1,208	-686	74	3,056
Year 5	1,208	-727	92	3,629
Year 6	1,208	-771	109	4,175
Year 7	1,208	-816	125	4,691
Year 8	1,208	-864	141	5,175
Year 9	1,208	-915	155	5,623
Year 10	1,208	-968	169	6,032
Year 11	1,208	-1,024	181	6,397
Year 12	1,208	-1,082	192	6,715
Year 13	1,208	-1,143	201	6,981
Year 14	1,208	-1,208	209	7,191
Year 15	1,208	-1,275	216	7,339
Year 16	1,208	-1,346	220	7,421
Year 17	1,208	-1,421	223	7,431
Year 18	1,208	-1,499	223	7,362
Year 19	1,208	-1,581	221	7,210

	PAIR 1 with 1 year delay			
	Ist House	2nd House	Net Interest	Cumulative CF
Year 20	1,208	-1,667	216	6,967
Year 21	1,208	-1,758	209	6,626
Year 22	1,208	-1,853	199	6,179
Year 23	1,208	-1,953	185	5,619
Year 24	1,208	-2,058	169	4,938
Year 25	1,208	-2,168	148	4,126
Year 26	1,208	-2,283	124	3,174
Year 27	1,208	4,509	95	8,986
Year 28	1,208	4,509	270	14,973
Year 29	1,208	4,509	449	21,139
Year 30	1,208	4,509	634	27,490

Comparing the figures we see that after 30 years you accumulate £31,100 when you purchase a property in the same year, and £27,490 when you purchase with a 1 year delay. The one year delay does not affect the final outcome to a great extent.

Key points from the chapter

- **Property investment should be made in pairs. This is the secret of Temperley's Back to Back© Model. First buy a property on an interest only mortgage, then a property on a repayment mortgage. The cashflow from the first covers the lack of cashflow on the second.**
- **The purchases must be done in the order of first purchase a property with an interest only mortgage, then purchase a property with a repayment mortgage.**
- **At the end of the mortgage term on the second property you will own the property outright..**

CHAPTER 8

TAX FOR INDIVIDUALS

Income Tax

Broadly speaking you will pay tax on the profit above. The exact amount depends on your personal situation. If your income in 2007 is already more than £39,826 you will pay tax at 40%. Between £7,546 and £39,825 the tax rate is 22%. If you have already used up your personal allowances with a day time job you will pay a straight percentage such as 40% on the rental profit.

It is possible to make a loss, but beware! The loss can only be offset against other rental income, not income from other sources such as salary.

Expenses and charges to reduce tax

You can claim expenses and charges related to the properties. Examples of expenses that can be claimed are mortgage interest, stationery, telephone, travel, buildings insurance, repairs and agents' fees.

Charging mileage

The current mileage rate that can be reimbursed is 40p per mile. There is a maximum mileage of 10,000 miles after which 25p can be claimed.

Wear and Tear Allowance

For furnished property there is also the possibility to claim wear and tear allowance as a deduction. This is 10% of the rental income on a property. This is claimed instead of taking a deduction for repairs.

Capital Gains Tax

There is no Capital Gains Tax to pay until you sell the property. This is a complex area and many factors determine how much tax is due, including length of ownership, whether you have lived in the property. There is an annual exemption of £9,200 (so £18.400 for a couple who have bought a property in joint names). Fortunately, we do not need to consider this as the strategy is to hold property and not to sell.

However, a better strategy is to not sell the property at all, but just increase the mortgage. If the property has risen in value from £100,000 to £200,000, you might well be able to raise an additional £60,000 quite easily which would enable you to keep the property too. Depending on what you do with the funds raised the interest might be tax deductible as well.

Key points from the chapter

- The tax situation of each individual is different. Before you decide what strategy you are going to follow (buy and sell or buy and hold for renting) you should have an idea of how tax affects you. If in doubt seek professional advice from an accountant.

- Selling a property that you own as a buy to let is not usually the best option as you have to pay tax on the profits. There may be better options depending on your own situation and what you want to do with the cash raised.

CHAPTER 9

OTHER PROPERTY INVESTMENT STRATEGIES

Instead of Buy to Let you could also consider a strategy of Buying, Renovating and Selling.

Consider the following scenario:

You purchase a property that needs some work doing on it. Naturally you purchase this at a price that is less than a property in the same area which does not need any work. The purchase process, work and selling process will take a year to complete. You are only buying and selling one property each year.

The cost of the property is £100,000 but the property needs £10,000 of work doing on it. I have assumed that the added value of the work is twice what the renovation cost, so every pound spent adds two pounds onto the property. *(this may not be the case in real life of course).*

The Purchase Costs

Purchase price		£100,000.00
Deposit	10%	£10,000.00
Mortgage		£90,000.00
Stamp duty		£0.00
Legal fees		£500.00
Searches		£450.00
Lenders fees		£199.00
Survey		£500.00
Total cash invested		**£11,649.00**

The Borrowing Costs

Interest rate	5.50%	
Interest per month		£412.50
Interest over 6 months		£2,475.00
Interest over 1 year		£4,950.00

The Preparation for Sale Costs

Refurbishment costs		£10,000.00
Estate agents fee	2%	£2,600.00
Legal fees		£500.00
Total Selling Costs		£13,100.00

The Sales Amount

Increase of	10%	£10,000.00	
Increase in value from refurbishment work			£20,000.00
Selling price			£130,000.00

Capital Gains Tax

Increase of	£30,000.00
less annual allowance	-£9,200.00
Tax @ 40%	£3,460.40

Profit and loss account

Sales price		£130,000.00
less amount borrowed		£90,000.00
less costs	stamp duty	£0.00
	legal fees on purchase	£500.00
	survey fees	£500.00
	refurbishment costs	£10,000.00
	mortgage interest	£4,950.00
	estate agent fees	£2,600.00
	legal fees on sale	£500.00
	tax	£3,460.40
	cash received	**£17,489.60**
	less investment	£10,000.00
	cash generated	£7,489.60

The return generated is good (£7,490) but consider the following:

- This is a simple example and there may well be other costs

- The return is high because there is an exemption of £9,200 from capital gains tax.

- The amount of cash received needs to provide a satisfactory margin. For example, building estimates are notoriously unreliable as are building timetables. The building cost of £10,000 may suddenly become £15,000 particularly if hidden defects are brought to light and need to be fixed.

- If you are a builder or are capable of doing the work yourself then the situation is different, but for the average person they are reliant on the work of others and the judgment of what needs to be done by others.

- If you are repairing 2 properties the return on the second is dramatically reduced because the tax rate is 40% on the profits of the second. (or if you are selling 2 finished rebuilding projects in the same tax year). This would give cash generated of £3,809 on the second property which leaves little room for error. This is why I do not favour this strategy – unless you are a builder, too much can go wrong and you end up out of pocket.

- However, you need to be able to finance the deposit (£10,000) and the renovation work (£10,000) as well as the monthly interest payments (£4,950) Legal and survey fees (£1,649) giving a total of £26,599 cash that needs to be available before you receive any cash return.

- Assuming you can finance the project you will receive the cash after a short period of time which is attractive.

The Purchase Costs

Purchase price		£100,000.00
Deposit	10%	£10,000.00
Mortgage		£90,000.00
Stamp duty		£0.00
Legal fees		£500.00
Searches		£450.00
Lenders fees		£199.00
Survey		£500.00
Total cash invested		**£11,649.00**

The Borrowing Costs

Interest rate	5.50%	
Interest per month		£412.50
Interest over 6 months		£2,475.00
Interest over 1 year		£4,950.00

The Preparation for Sale Costs

Refurbishment costs		£10,000.00
Estate agents fee	2%	£2,600.00
Legal fees		£500.00
Total Selling Costs		£13,100.00

The Sales Amount

Increase of	10%	£10,000.00	
Increase in value from refurbishment work			£20,000.00

Selling price		£130,000.00

Capital Gains Tax

Increase of		£30,000.00
Tax @ 40%		£7,140.40

Profit and loss account		
Sales price		£130,000.00
less amount borrowed		£90,000.00
less costs	stamp duty	£0.00
	legal fees on purchase	£500.00
	survey fees	£500.00
	refurbishment costs	£10,000.00
	mortgage interest	£4,950.00
	estate agent fees	£2,600.00
	legal fees on sale	£500.00
	tax	£7,140.40
	cash received	£13,809.60
	less investment	£10,000.00
	cash generated	**£3,809.60**

The tax bill can be reduced if a couple (or two people) purchases the property jointly. The return on a single property would be £11,170. This does reduce the risk by a considerable percentage.

Let us examine what happens if the property costs more than £125,000, where **stamp duty** becomes payable.

The Purchase Costs

Purchase price		£130,000.00
Deposit	10%	£13,000.00
Mortgage		£117,000.00
Stamp duty	**1%**	**£1,300.00**
Legal fees		£500.00
Searches		£450.00
Lenders fees		£199.00
Survey		£500.00
Total cash invested		**£15,949.00**

The Borrowing Costs

Interest rate	5.50%	
Interest per month		£536.25
Interest over 6 months		£3,217.50
Interest over 1 year		£6,435.00

The Preparation for Sale Costs

Refurbishment costs		£10,000.00
Estate agents fee	2%	£3,260.00
Legal fees		£500.00
Total Selling Costs		£13,760.00

The Sales Amount

Increase of	10%	£13,000.00	
Increase in value from refurbishment work			£20,000.00
Selling price			£163,000.00

Capital Gains Tax

Increase of	£33,000.00
less annual allowance	-£9,200.00
Tax @ 40%	£4,140.40

Profit and loss account

Sales price		£163,000.00
less amount borrowed		£117,000.00
less costs	**stamp duty**	**£1,300.00**
	legal fees on purchase	£500.00
	survey fees	£500.00
	refurbishment costs	£10,000.00
	mortgage interest	£6,435.00
	estate agent fees	£3,260.00
	legal fees on sale	£500.00
	tax	£4,140.40
	cash received	£19,364.60
	less investment	£13,000.00
	cash generated	£6,364.60

The cash generated falls to £6,365 (from £7,490) and the amount of finance that has to be provided by the investor increases by £1,300 to £27,900.
50

The examples given above are simple examples. There are a number of variables.

- **Purchase price:** the assumption is that the price is less than the market value. Therefore it follows that the purchase price should be the market value of a similar property in good condition less the cost of the renovation less a profit element.

- **Renovation costs:** Accurately estimating the cost of the renovation work and the time taken to complete it are key elements.

- **Time to complete:** The time affects how much interest is paid. The longer the time period the higher the interest and the less the eventual profit.

- **Selling price after renovation:** for this strategy to work you must be able to sell the property for more that you paid for it. It therefore follows that when prices are increasing this strategy should work well, but when prices are falling this strategy needs to be carefully controlled.

Key points from the chapter

- **Buying and holding (Buy to Let) is not the only way to make money from residential property. You can pursue a strategy of buying and selling which can become self-financing after a few years.**

- **However, this strategy only works where three conditions are met:**
  - **you purchase below the market price,**
  - **you accurately estimate the cost of renovations (if any) and can control these costs**
  - **you can sell the property for more than you paid (so may not work in a period when house prices are going down)**

CHAPTER 10

INCORPORATION – BUYING VIA A LIMITED COMPANY

There is a brief summary in the first half of this chapter about forming and running a company with more detail later. The advantages of using a company are lower taxes but more administration. However, you can pay a professional to do the accounting and company secretarial side at a reasonable cost so the complications should not deter you.

Incorporation means that you form a company to purchase property instead of buying it yourself. The difference is that the company owns the property, not you; you own the company (or part of the company) as a shareholder. The key point to recognise is that a company is a separate entity. This means that it is a legal person in its own right. It is separate from those who own or run it, and has 'limited liability'. Limited liability gives the owners of the company (its shareholders) protection if the company fails. This means that if a company is put into liquidation, the people who own the company will only be required to pay what they have already paid or agreed to pay towards settling its debts.

Advantages of buying property via a company

Simply put, buying property via a company is good if you want to hold the property and accumulate cash over a long term. It is not good if you want to buy and sell property over a short term. This is primarily because as an individual you have an annual exemption for capital gains of £9,200 (£18,400 for a couple) which is not available to a company.

The other advantage that a company has is that it pays less tax than an individual. The current rate of corporation tax for small companies (the company's version of income tax) is just 20%. This compares favourably to the main income tax rates for individuals of 22% and 40%.

Not only does a company pay less tax on its profits but it can offset more expenses than an individual. The Inland Revenue does not consider investing in property as a trade, but as a business. While trying not to laugh about the semantics the differences are largely that as an individual you cannot generally offset the expenses of going to see a property you do not own or do not eventually buy, whilst a company can. This may not sound like much until you consider that if you charge the company 40p per mile (the maximum tax free reimbursement currently allowed by the Inland

Revenue) the costs saved can mount up. For example a trip to Liverpool from London to look at some prospective properties involving a return journey of 800 miles would enable a company to offset £320.

Setting up and running a company

This is the easy part! You can set up a company in as little as 30 minutes via the internet. Essentially the company needs to keep records , primarily a set of accounts and to file an annual return and a tax return. You need a minimum of one shareholder, although more than one is usual, one director, and a company secretary. The director, or directors, must manage the company's affairs in accordance with its articles of association and the law. The company secretary is the chief administrator of the company. A sole director cannot also be the secretary, so appoint your wife/husband/ significant other/son/ daughter/father/mother etc. as the other director so you can be the company secretary. The company secretary of a private limited company needs no formal qualifications.

Duties of a Company Secretary

The company secretary usually undertakes the following duties:

1.   **Maintaining the statutory registers.** These are:

- the register of members (section 352);

- the register of directors and secretaries (section 288);

- the register of directors' interests (section 325);

- the register of charges (section 407 or 422 for Scottish companies)

2.   **Ensuring that statutory forms are filed promptly.** You cannot simply send a letter to notify the Registrar that you wish to change the situation of the company's registered office or that changes have occurred among directors or secretaries or their particulars. You should normally use forms 287 and 288a, b or c as appropriate. You may also use the annual return Form 363s in some circumstances if the return is due at the convenient time. Changes of directors' and secretaries' details must be notified within 14 days.

3.   **Providing members and auditors with notice of meetings.** You must give them 21 days written notice of an annual general meeting. You must

give them 14 days written notice of a meeting which is neither an annual general meeting or a meeting to pass a special resolution.

4.   Sending the Registrar copies of resolutions and agreements. You must send the Registrar copies of every resolution or agreement to which section 380 applies, for example special and extraordinary resolutions, within 15 days of them being passed.

5.   Supplying a copy of the accounts to every member of the company, every debenture holder and every person who is entitled to receive notice of general meetings - also copies demanded by anyone under section 239 of the Act. You must send accounts at least 21 days before a meeting at which they are to be laid - see section 238 of the Act.

6.   Keeping, or arranging for the keeping, of minutes of directors' meetings and general meetings.

7.   Ensuring that people entitled to do so can inspect company records. For example, members of the company and members of the public are entitled to a copy of the company's register of members, and members of the company are entitled to inspect the minutes of its general meetings and to have copies of these minutes.

8.   Custody and use of the company seal. Companies no longer need to have a company seal, but if they do, the secretary is usually responsible for its custody and use. (Company seals can be bought from legal stationers and company formation agents.)

What you have to send to Companies House

Company directors and secretaries are responsible for delivering information to the Registrar. There are over 200 forms that companies could file. Below are the most common forms and documents that companies will use.

1. Accounts

All limited companies, whether trading or not, must keep accounting records and file accounts for each accounting period with the Registrar.

Unless a company is claiming exemption as a medium-sized, small, audit-exempt or dormant company, the accounts will include:

- a directors' report signed by a director or the company secretary;

- a balance sheet signed by a director;

- a profit and loss account (or income and expenditure account if the company is not trading for profit);

- an auditors' report signed by the auditor;

- notes to the accounts; and

- group accounts (if appropriate).

Accounts must be produced to a standard that can be scanned to reproduce electronically.

Directors are personally responsible for ensuring that accounts are prepared and delivered to Companies House.

2. Annual returns (Form 363)

The company must submit an annual return (Forms 363a or 363s) every year to Companies House. **The good news is this is the easy part as Companies House sends you a filled out form every year and you just sign it if there are no changes.** The form has to be signed and returned within 28 days but can be submitted online.

An annual return is a snapshot of general information about a company's directors and secretary, registered office address, shareholders and share capital. Note that annual returns are quite separate from annual accounts.

Ensure that you use the appropriate trade code:

Trade Code Group K - Real Estate, Renting & Business

7011 Development & sell real estate

7012 Buying & sell own real estate

7020 Letting of own property

7031 Real estate agencies

7032 Manage real estate, fee or contract

Note: the trade code is actually quite important. Some lenders will not lend to a company to buy property if it has the 'wrong' trade code, i.e. one outside the list above. My suggestion is to use codes 7012 and 7032.

Companies House Online Filing

For a government department, **Companies House is excellent**. Not only do they actually answer the telephone, the people who answer the telephone are knowledgeable and helpful. **Their website is good** too, and filing information online is easy. (It's cheaper too – manual filing of the annual return costs £30 whereas online filing costs £15) Online filing can be done between 7 am and midnight, Monday to Saturday.

The weblink is https://ewf.companieshouse.gov.uk/

Below are some of the screens you will see if you decide to file online.

1. The welcome screen

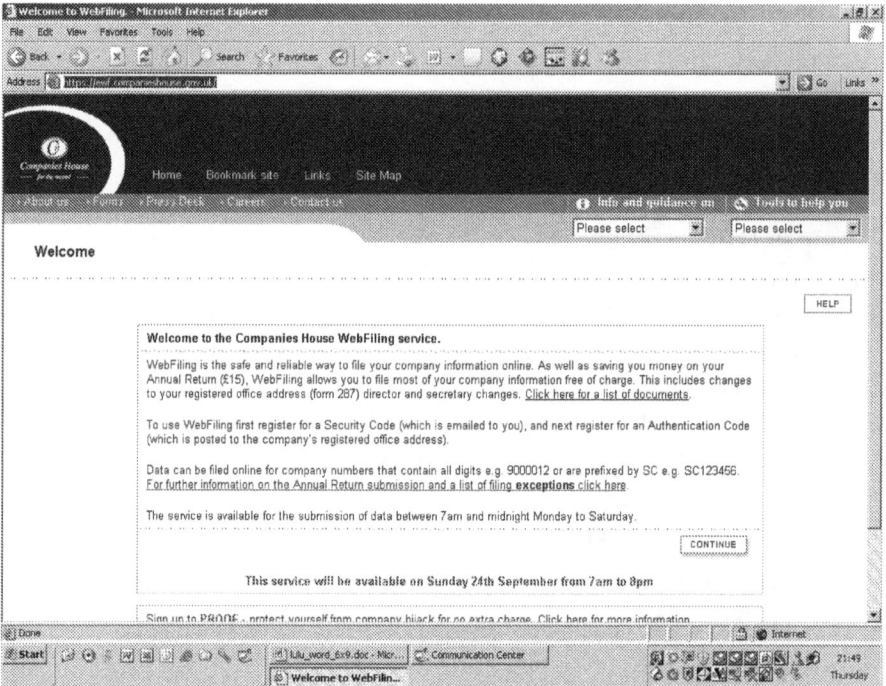

You have to pre-register and Companies House will send you an Security Code by email and an Authentication code by mail. You need both these bits of information to use the online service.

2. The Login Page

You need the email address and security code. The email address is the same one that you used to request online filing, but it can be changed once you have logged in.

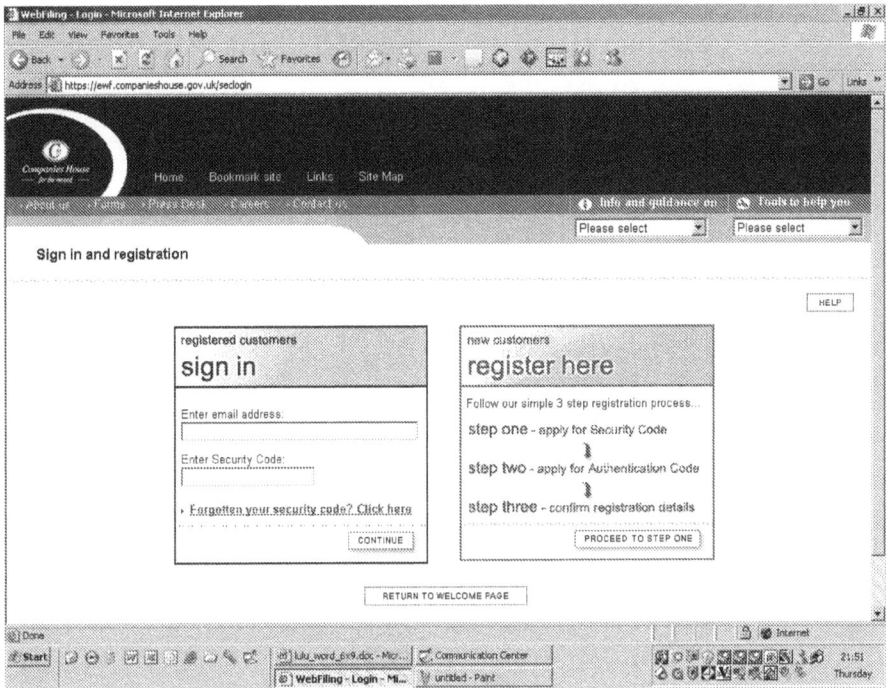

3. The second screen of the sign in. Here you need the company number and the Authentication code. .

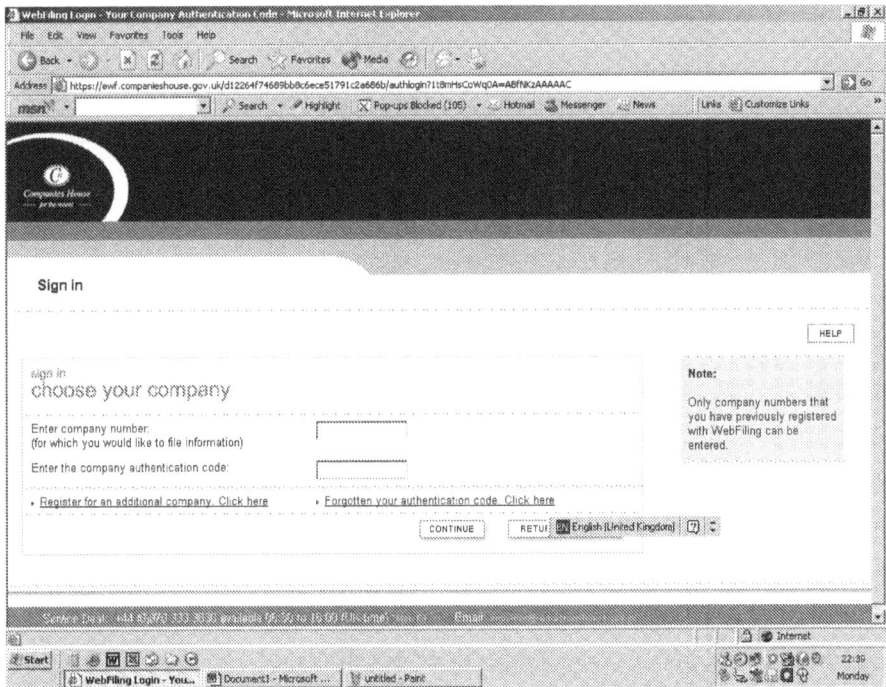

4. Menu screen

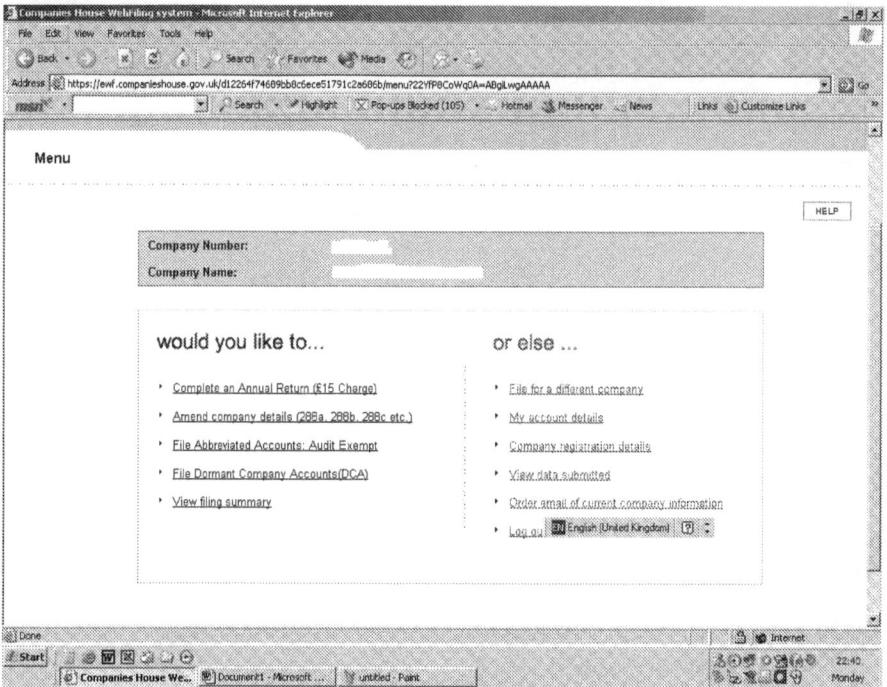

Items on the menu include:

- File the annual return – have a debit card ready!

- Amend company details (e.g. change of directors and their details)

- File accounts

3. Change of accounting reference date - Form 225

Every company has an accounting reference date, which is the date to which the company's accounts are prepared each year. This date can be changed using Form 225.

4. Change of registered office - Form 287

It is important to keep Companies House informed of the location of your registered office. All formal communications are sent there.

Every company must have a registered office. It is the 'home' of the company to which all official documents, notices and court papers have to be sent by law. The address must be a physical location, not just a post office box. This is because people have the right to visit your office to inspect certain registers and documents, and to deliver documents by hand.

You can change your registered office address by sending a completed Form 287 to the Registrar. The change becomes legally effective only when the form has been registered with Companies House.

5. Change of directors and secretary and their details - Forms 288

There are three types of Form 288.

Form 288(a) is used for the appointment of an officer.

Form 288(b) is used for an officer ceasing to act (resignation, removal, death etc).

Form 288(c) is used for a change in details of an officer, for example, a change of name or new residential address.

All changes to directors' and secretary's details must be sent to the Registrar within 14 days of the change.

6. Allotments of shares - Form 88(2)

This form should be sent to Companies House within one month of the shares being allotted.

7. Resolutions

Copies of any special or extraordinary resolutions and certain types of ordinary resolutions, need to be sent to Companies House within 15 days of them being passed by the company. When a resolution alters the memorandum or articles of a company, a copy of the amended document must also be sent in at the same time as the resolution.

There is no special form to complete but the document must be produced to a standard that can be scanned and reproduced electronically.

8. Mortgages and charges

Details of any mortgage or charge created by the company must be sent to Companies House within 21 days. Usually the lawyers of the mortgage company will do this (as the charge registration is there to protect the creditors).

The address for sending documents to is:

The Registrar of Companies

Companies House

Crown Way

Cardiff CF14 3UZ

Wales

Note that you cannot send documents by fax to Companies House.

Accounts – keeping the books

Unless you are an accountant or bookkeeper, get them prepared by a professional. Costs start from £200 per year. Don't forget to keep receipts for all expenditure! You will need to submit the accounts with the tax return and send a set to Companies House. The time limits are 10 months after the end of the accounting reference period. So if your company's year end is 31st. December the accounts must be submitted by the end of the following October. Given that you are likely to have a maximum of 10 properties (general lending criteria) the deadline is not too onerous. There is a fine for late accounts.

The Inland Revenue will send you a tax return with a request for the accounts before the 10 months so it is advisable to have the accounts prepared earlier rather than later.

Generally, accounts must include:

- a profit and loss account;
- a balance sheet signed by a director;
- an auditors' report signed by the auditor (but see below);
- a directors' report signed by a director or the secretary of the company;
- notes to the accounts

Auditors

Your company will qualify as a "small company" and therefore will not need an annual audit. To qualify for audit exemption as a small company, the company must:

- qualify as small;
- have a turnover of not more than £5.6 million; and
- have a balance sheet total of not more than £2.8 million.

Being a director

Anybody can be a company director subject to certain qualifications:

- the person must not have been disqualified by a court from acting as a company director (unless he or she has been given leave (permission) to act by a court for a particular company);
- the person must not be an undischarged bankrupt (except with leave of the court);

Every company director has a personal responsibility to ensure that statutory documents are delivered to the Registrar as and when required by the Act. In particular:

- accounts (only for limited companies);
- annual returns (Form 363);
- notice of change of directors or secretaries or in their particulars (Forms 288a/b/c); and
- notice of change of registered office (Form 287).

Further information is available from the Companies House Website
http://www.companieshouse.gov.uk/about/guidance.shtml

The Inland Revenue

You need to inform the Inland Revenue that you have formed a company. Often the Revenue writes to you once you have formed the company, but do not rely on this. You can get the address and telephone number of your local office from the Inland Revenue website.

Tax Return

Unless you are an accountant, get the company tax return prepared by a professional. You will need to submit the tax return within 12 months of the end of the accounting period.

The Golden Rule with companies

The Golden Rule is to **keep everything simple**. Your company is not going to be a large company with an army of administrators and expensive professional advisors to take care of everything. This means that the company avoids:

- having employees (directors are not employees)
- making payments (no bonuses, no salaries – there are no employees – no dividends)
- no company cars
- being large enough to need to register for VAT

REMEMBER – THERE IS NO PROFIT IN ADMINISTRATION

Key points from the chapter

- **Buying via a limited company can make more money in the long run because the lower tax rates enables the company to generate more cash.**
- **If you use a company keep it simple.**
- **Most people could be a company director, and probably manage being the company secretary** (but it is not expensive to use a professional).
- **Get the annual accounts prepared by a professional.**

CHAPTER 11

TAX FOR COMPANIES

Warning - tax rates do change:

In 2005 the tax rate for small companies with profits of less than £10,000 per year was 0%, in 2006 it was 19%, in 2007 it is 20%, in 2008 it will be 21%, and in 2009 it will be 22%! Consequently, before you form a company, check what the latest rate is and calculate whether it still makes sense to use a company or not. You should take specialist advice before you form a company.

Corporation tax. In 2007 profits are taxed at 20% for small companies.

VAT When your turnover (or rental income) reaches £64,000 you must register for VAT. As the VAT will either be added onto your invoices, thus increasing the final amount by 17.5% giving a monthly rental charge to tenants of £705 (instead of £600). **As any tenant who cannot recover the VAT is unlikely to rent your property, it is important not to let the company get too big!** Although technically if you register for VAT you can recover VAT from your expenses this is not worth doing because if your expenses are more than your rent you will be making a loss, and secondly there is a lot of complicated paperwork to do, such as a VAT return. There are also likely to be few expenses where you can actually recover the VAT.

REMEMBER – THERE IS NO PROFIT IN ADMINISTRATION

Charging mileage

The current mileage rate that can be reimbursed is 40p per mile. Claiming this is much simpler than buying a company car. There is a maximum mileage of 10,000 miles, after which only 25p can be claimed.

TAKING MONEY OUT OF THE COMPANY

It is important to realise that just because you own the shares in the company, the money in the company's bank account belongs to the company and not to you. There are rules designed to protect creditors and prevent the company running out of money. This is a complex area and professional advice should be sought for your individual circumstances.

The main ways to take money out of the company all have tax consequences and are therefore a complication. These are:

- Paying a salary
- Paying a dividend

1.   Paying a salary

Until all mortgages have been paid off I don't recommend taking any money out of the company. The salary will be added onto your existing salary for tax purposes, probably at 40%, the company will pay National Insurance at 12.8%, and there is the administration involved.

REMEMBER – THERE IS NO PROFIT IN ADMINISTRATION

When you have retired, you may be able to take the salary at a lower tax rate of 22%. You may have even moved overseas where the tax rates are lower.

2.   Paying a dividend to yourself

Until all mortgages have been paid off I don't recommend taking any money out of the company at all. A dividend payment will generate a 19% tax charge and the dividend is added to your income. However, there is no National Insurance to pay on dividends.

So how do I take money out of the company?

The short answer is that you don't!

Let me explain. The company is a great low-tax savings vehicle. First the tax rate is low at 20%, secondly there are lots of expenses the company can claim to lower this tax bill.

If you must take money out of a company

There are two good ways to take money out of the company:

1.   as a repayment of a loan

2.   on retirement, when you may move from a 40% tax bracket to a 22% tax bracket. (in this option you defer the tax you pay, and may end up paying it a lower rate)

Repayment of a loan

Making an interest free loan to the company is an efficient way to receive money back later. When a property is purchased there is an amount which is not covered by the mortgage. You can put this money into the company by issuing shares or as a loan. I suggest an interest free loan because a loan with interest means that the interest will be taxed (i.e. a complication). However, the capital repayment can take place at any time. The capital repayments of the investments on 8 properties would be £127,992, (assuming the property cost is £100,000 and 15% is used as a deposit – more details in the example on page 68) which spread over 5 years at retirement would give a **tax free repayment** 'income' of £25,598 per year for 5 years. Not bad indeed! You will only need to pay tax once you start paying a salary when the capital repayments are exhausted.

You also have the possibility outside of the company to borrow the money you put into the property company and claim tax relief for the interest paid.

Key points from the chapter
- **Don't take the money out of a company until you retire. Buying property via a limited company is a great way to supplement a pension.**
- **You need to get specialist advice from your accountant before you set up a company.**
- **You need to get specialist advice from your accountant before you take money out of a company.**

CHAPTER 12

KEY DIFFERENCES BETWEEN BUYING AS AN INDIVIDUAL AND BUYING AS A COMPANY

	Individual	Company
Tax on profit	22% or 40%	20%
Allowances	Personal allowance of £5,035	No personal allowances
Administration		Company law must be followed, with annual meetings, send an annual return to Companies House
Obtaining the cash	No restrictions	Consideration needs to be given as to how to take the money out of the company
Raising the finance	Usually can borrow 90% of the property value Wide choice of lenders	Usually a maximum of 85% of the property value can be borrowed. The interest rate is often higher. Restricted choice of lenders Difficult to borrow for properties worth less than £50,000
Capital Gains Tax	Annual exemption of £8,800 (£17,600 for a couple)	No annual exemption
Ownership of the property	You as an individual own the property in your own name.	The company owns the property. You own (shares in) the company

When comparing cashflows the limited company makes more money over the long term. This is mainly because the company tax rate is lower (20%) than the tax rate on individuals (40%) so you can accumulate more cash.

Comparison of cumulative cashflow between buying via a company and buying as an individual

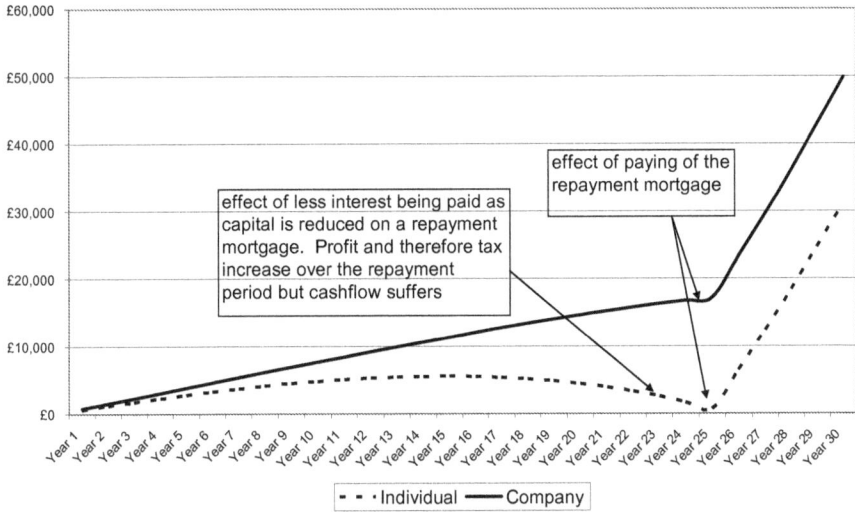

effect of less interest being paid as capital is reduced on a repayment mortgage. Profit and therefore tax increase over the repayment period but cashflow suffers

effect of paying of the repayment mortgage

- - -Individual ——Company

CHAPTER 13

APPLYING TEMPERLEY'S BACK TO BACK© MODEL TO A LIMITED COMPANY

At first sight applying the Back to Back© Model seems to be the same. However, there are some subtle differences. From the table above you can see that companies can borrow less, and pay more for their borrowing. However, companies pay less tax on profits.

This affects the Back to Back© Model. Using the same data as above, except for the deposit percentage and the interest rate, the Back to Back© Model generates the following.

Purchase Price of Property	£100,000
Deposit %	15%
Deposit £	£15,000
Legal fees	£400
Survey	£400
Stamp duty	Nil
Mortgage arrangement fee	£199
Refurbishment	Nil
Furniture	Nil
Rental Income per month	£550
Rental Income per year	£6,600
Agents Fees	£846
Insurance	£80
Repairs	£150
Rate of interest	6%
Mortgage Interest	£5,100

Using the figures above you can calculate the profit or loss on the property.

Rental Income	6,600
Expenses	6,106
Profit	**495**

Profit is therefore £495 per year.

This gives a return of 3.1%

(Profit of £495 / Investment of £15,999 x 100)

Tax is 20% (£99) giving an after tax profit of £396.

Let's compare this to how the same investment would calculate for an individual.

Company			**Individual**		
Property Price		100,000	Property Price		100,000
Deposit 15%		15,000	Deposit 10%		10,000
Legal fees		400	Legal fees		400
Survey fees		400	Survey fees		400
Refurbishment		199	Refurbishment		199
	Total Investment	**15,999**		**Total Investment**	**10,999**
Mortgage amount		85,000	Mortgage amount		90,000
Rent per month	600		Rent per month	600	
Annual Rental		7,200	Annual Rental		7,200
Mortgage interest @ 5.5%		-4,675	Mortgage interest @ 5%		-4,500
Insurance		-80	Insurance		-80
Repairs		-150	Repairs		-150
Agent fee		-846	Agent fee		-846
	Annual profit	**1,449**		**Annual profit**	**1,624**
Tax		290	Tax		650
Profit after tax		1,159	Profit after tax		974
	Return on investment	**7.2%**		**Return on investment**	**8.9%**

On first sight it seems as if buying via a company does not generate the best return, (this is because a company needs to put down a higher deposit than an individual) but notice that the **cash generated** is higher with a company than for an individual. However, over time, with the lower tax rate that a company suffers, the retained cashflows are significantly higher.

	COMPANY			INDIVIDUAL		
Year	Annual inflow	Net Interest	Cumulative Cashflow	Annual inflow	Net Interest	Cumulative Cashflow
1	1,159		1,159	974		974
2	2,318	47	2,365	1,949	29	1,978
3	3,525	96	3,620	2,952	59	3,012
4	4,780	147	4,926	3,986	90	4,077
5	6,085	200	6,285	5,051	122	5,173
6	7,444	255	7,699	6,148	155	6,303
7	8,858	312	9,170	7,277	189	7,466
8	10,329	371	10,700	8,441	224	8,665
9	11,859	433	12,293	9,639	260	9,899
10	13,452	498	13,950	10,873	297	11,170
11	15,109	565	15,674	12,145	335	12,480
12	16,833	635	17,468	13,454	374	13,829
13	18,627	707	19,335	14,803	415	15,218
14	20,494	783	21,277	16,192	457	16,649
15	22,436	862	23,298	17,623	499	18,123
16	24,457	944	25,401	19,097	544	19,641
17	26,560	1,029	27,588	20,615	589	21,204
18	28,748	1,117	29,865	22,179	636	22,815
19	31,024	1,210	32,234	23,789	684	24,474
20	33,393	1,305	34,698	25,448	734	26,182
21	35,858	1,405	37,263	27,157	785	27,942
22	38,422	1,509	39,931	28,917	838	29,755
23	41,090	1,617	42,708	30,729	893	31,622
24	43,867	1,730	45,596	32,596	949	33,545
25	46,756	1,847	48,602	34,520	1,006	35,526

In the example above, nearly 40% more cash is generated by a company than for an individual.

Applying Temperley's Back to Back© Model

Simply put, you purchase property in pairs up to the threshold of VAT, which is currently £64,000. Using the figures above this would indicate 8 properties should be purchased with annual rental of £7,200.

The key here is exactly the same as the situation where a property is purchased in the name of an individual, i.e. purchase the first property in the pair with an interest only mortgage, and the second property with a repayment mortgage. Let's see what happens over 25 years for the first pair. The figures are after-tax cashflows.

	Interest Only	Repayment	Net interest	Cumulative Cashflow
Year 1	1,174	-429	0	730
Year 2	1,174	-449	22	1,462
Year 3	1,174	-470	44	2,195
Year 4	1,174	-491	66	2,929
Year 5	1,174	-514	88	3,662
Year 6	1,174	-538	110	4,393
Year 7	1,174	-563	132	5,122
Year 8	1,174	-589	154	5,845
Year 9	1,174	-617	175	6,563
Year 10	1,174	-646	197	7,274
Year 11	1,174	-676	218	7,976
Year 12	1,174	-708	239	8,666
Year 13	1,174	-741	260	9,344
Year 14	1,174	-776	280	10,007
Year 15	1,174	-813	300	10,653
Year 16	1,174	-852	320	11,280
Year 17	1,174	-893	338	11,884
Year 18	1,174	-936	357	12,464
Year 19	1,174	-981	374	13,017
Year 20	1,174	-1,028	391	13,539
Year 21	1,174	-1,077	406	14,027
Year 22	1,174	-1,129	421	14,478
Year 23	1,174	-1,184	434	14,887
Year 24	1,174	-1,241	447	15,252
Year 25	1,174	-1,301	458	15,567

When year 25 is over the second property in the first pair has been paid off. The consequence of this is that in year 26 there is no interest deduction but instead a lot of cash is generated.

Year 26 gives the following

	Interest Only	Repayment	Net Interest	Cumulative cashflow
Year 26	1,174	4,454	467	21,647

As you can see, once the mortgage is paid off on the property with the repayment mortgage the cashflows jump.

The cashflow will not by itself enable the investor to buy the second property from retained profits. However, if other pairs of property are added there will be enough cash to buy off at least one of the properties purchased with an interest only mortgage. Adding a second pair a year later and a third pair a year after that gives the following.

| | PAIR 1 + PAIR 2 + PAIR 3 | | | |
	1ST PAIR	2ND PAIR	3RD PAIR	CUMULATIVE
YEAR 1	730			730
YEAR 2	732	730		2,191
YEAR 3	733	732	730	4,387
YEAR 4	734	733	732	6,586
YEAR 5	733	734	733	8,786
YEAR 6	731	733	734	10,984
YEAR 7	728	731	733	13,177
YEAR 8	724	728	731	15,360
YEAR 9	718	724	728	17,531
YEAR 10	711	718	724	19,683
YEAR 11	702	711	718	21,813
YEAR 12	691	702	711	23,916
YEAR 13	678	691	702	25,986
YEAR 14	663	678	691	28,018
YEAR 15	646	663	678	30,004
YEAR 16	627	646	663	31,940
YEAR 17	605	627	646	33,817
YEAR 18	580	605	627	35,628
YEAR 19	553	580	605	37,365
YEAR 20	522	553	580	39,020
YEAR 21	488	522	553	40,582
YEAR 22	451	488	522	42,043
YEAR 23	410	451	488	43,392
YEAR 24	365	410	451	44,617
YEAR 25	315	365	410	45,707
YEAR 26	6,080	315	365	52,467
YEAR 27	6,262	6,080	315	65,125
YEAR 28	6,450	6,262	6,080	83,917
YEAR 29	6,644	6,450	6,262	103,274
YEAR 30	6,843	6,644	6,450	123,211

What the table means

The repayment mortgage from the first pair is paid off in year 25. This means that in year 26 there are few expenses for the repayment mortgage property as there is no interest or capital repayment to make.

By year 29 there is enough cash generated to pay off the first interest only mortgage.

Key points from the chapter

- **Applying Temperley's Back to Back© Model to a company has to be done in exactly the same was as applying it for an individual. i.e. the first investment of a pair must be an interest only mortgage and the second a repayment mortgage.**
- **Using a company is a good method for accumulating cash because the tax rate for a company on its profits is less than the tax for an individual on his income.**
- **The cash retained can be used in the future to pay off one or more of the interest-only mortgages.**

CHAPTER 14

THE ULTIMATE STRATEGY

If Christmas came early in the Buy to Let Land, on the list of presents there would be a 100% mortgage (alongside other items such as tenants who always paid on time and cleaned up before they left a property). It is possible to (eventually) obtain a 100% mortgage, or even higher!

Here is how it works and why you would want it.

In this strategy you purchase a property in your own name. If prices rise you are able to re-mortgage the property for a larger amount. By putting the money raised from the increased mortgage into a property company you obtain tax relief.

The company then takes out a mortgage for 85% of the property value. The company uses the money you have put in as a deposit of 15%. (and don't forget that you put the money into the company as a loan so you can withdraw it later).

Congratulations! You have achieved the Holy Grail of a 100% mortgage. The obvious limitation is that you have to buy a property and wait for it to increase in value. Now comes the fun part.

Take one of the examples in Chapter 5 where you calculated the returns. Try to calculate the return with a zero investment and you'll get a strange answer (because you can't divide by zero). Try the same calculation with an investment of the legal and survey fees.

Example 1

Example 1 with £10% investment

Property Price		100,000
Deposit	10%	10,000
Legal fees		300
Survey fees		300
Refurbishment		2,000
	Total Investment	**12,600**
Mortgage amount		90,000
Rent per month	600	
Annual Rental		7,200
Mortgage interest @ 5%		-4,500
Insurance		-100
Repairs		-200
Agent fee		-846
	Annual profit	**1,554**
Return on investment (before tax)		**12%**

Example 1 with £100 investment

Property Price		100,000
Deposit		0
Legal fees		300
Survey fees		300
Refurbishment		2,000
	Total Investment	**2,600**
Mortgage amount		100,000
Rent per month	600	
Annual Rental		7,200
Mortgage interest @ 5%		-5,000
Insurance		-100
Repairs		-200
Agent fee		-846
	Annual profit	**1,054**
Return on investment (before tax)		**41%**

This being said, if a calculation shows a bad investment with a low return, using a 100% mortgage is not going to make the investment better. What the Ultimate strategy does is increase the return with a good investment but increase the loss with a bad investment. You have to have a good investment in the first place to make the ultimate strategy work successfully.

Example 1 with 10% investment

Property Price		125,000

Deposit	10%	12,500
Legal fees		300
Survey fees		300
Refurbishment		2,000
Furniture		1,500
Total Investment		**16,600**

Mortgage amount		112,500
Rent per month	500	

Annual Rental	6,000
Mortgage interest @ 5%	-5,625
Insurance	-100
Repairs	-200
Agent fee	-705
Annual profit	**-630**

Return on investment (before tax)	**-4%**

Example 1 with £100 investment

Property Price	125,000

Deposit	0
Legal fees	300
Survey fees	300
Refurbishment	2,000
Furniture	1,500
Total Investment	**4,100**

Mortgage amount		125,000
Rent per month	500	

Annual Rental	6,000
Mortgage interest @ 5%	-6,250
Insurance	-100
Repairs	-200
Agent fee	-705
Annual profit	**-1,255**

Return on investment (before tax)	**-31%**

Key points from the chapter

- The smaller amount of money you personally put into a project the better, because the returns will be greater and you are risking less of your own money.

CHAPTER 15

THE EFFECT OF INFLATION

Inflation can be your friend! OK, let me rephrase this. Moderate inflation can be your friend.

Let's have a look at how this can be with the following scenario.

If we assume that inflation is 2% this will affect all the items except mortgage interest. As we have seen over the past few years there have not been significant rises in interest rates whilst inflation has been low, so my assumption is that when inflation is low at around 2% the Bank of England has no need to raise interest rates.

This is important because the interest payments on a mortgage are the largest expense that a buy to let investor faces. However, if all other items (rent, insurance, repairs, agents fees) rise in line with inflation but the interest payments remain constant, the effect is dramatic.

The effects are shown below.

Cashflow when inflation is 2% and mortgage rate is constant

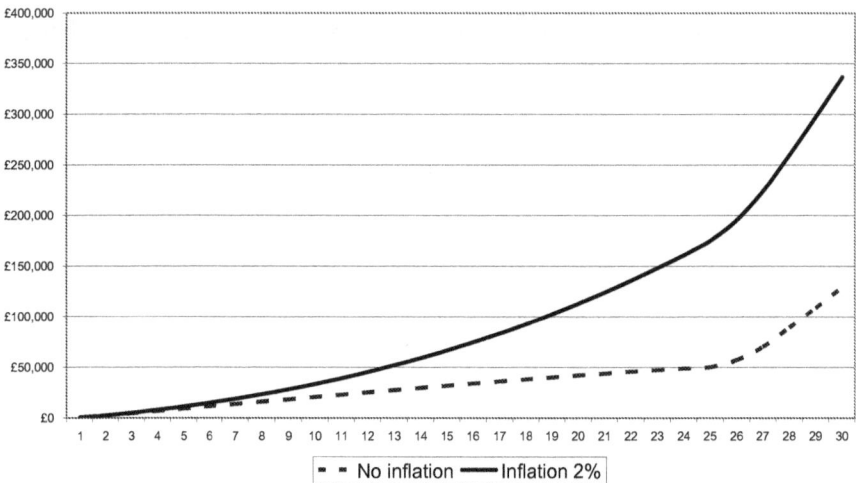

The amount borrowed remains constant. **This is the key point**. No matter what inflation does, the amount you have borrowed remains the same. So if inflation means that after 25 years the pound in your pocket is worth half what it was when you took out the loan, your debt has halved in real terms. However, rent keeps pace with inflation, and the mortgage debt shrinks, making it easier to pay off. Consequently you should be able to purchase the second or even third property that has been purchased on an interest only mortgage.

Below is the value of £100,000 at different inflation rates over 25 years

Year	2%	4%	6%
1	102,000	104,000	106,000
2	104,040	108,160	112,360
3	106,121	112,486	119,102
4	108,243	116,986	126,248
5	110,408	121,665	133,823
6	112,616	126,532	141,852
7	114,869	131,593	150,363
8	117,166	136,857	159,385
9	119,509	142,331	168,948
10	121,899	148,024	179,085
11	124,337	153,945	189,830
12	126,824	160,103	201,220
13	129,361	166,507	213,293
14	131,948	173,168	226,090
15	134,587	180,094	239,656
16	137,279	187,298	254,035
17	140,024	194,790	269,277
18	142,825	202,582	285,434
19	145,681	210,685	302,560
20	148,595	219,112	320,714
21	151,567	227,877	339,956
22	154,598	236,992	360,354
23	157,690	246,472	381,975
24	160,844	256,330	404,893
25	164,061	266,584	429,187

Alternatively, you can see the effects of inflation graphically:

Inflation at different rates

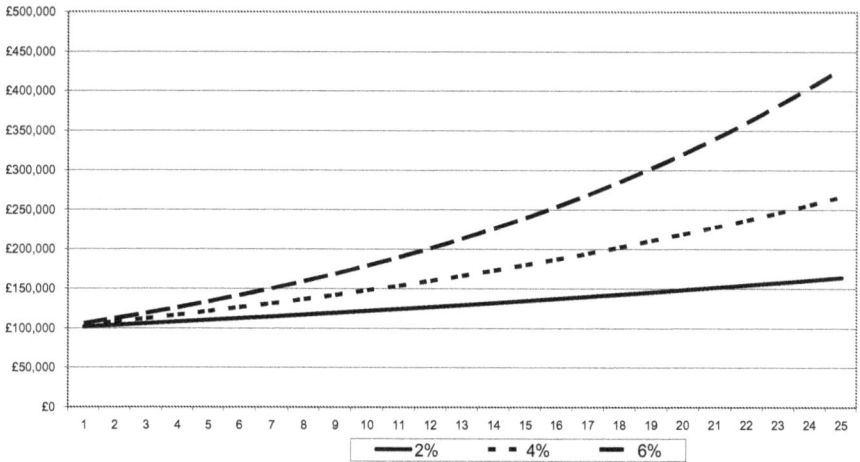

Clearly, you will be able to sell the property and repay the existing mortgage, even after paying capital gains tax. Note that what is left over will be worth less in 25 years time than it is in today's money.

Key points from the chapter

- **A little bit of inflation is good for you as a buy-to-let investor because rents increase but the mortgage stays the same.**

- **High inflation is unlikely to be good as rents will not rise as fast as inflation.**

CHAPTER 16

HOUSES VERSUS FLATS

There are an incredible amount of new flats being built at the moment. It is not difficult to understand why. From the builders' point of view, there is more profit per square foot as the density of housing is higher. Simply put, you can cram more people in.

For the buy to let investor, flats present a problem. They can be difficult to rent out in some areas, and indeed may cost more to purchase than an older terraced house.

More importantly however is the annual maintenance charge that comes with a flat, as well as the charge for ground rent. It is not uncommon for the annual service charge to be more than one thousand pounds. This is not only over-expensive, but significantly reduces the annual profit on a property.

To show you the effect of the service charge, let's compare the returns of a potential investment without and with a service charge of £500 per year.

Example 1 without service charge		
Property Price		100,000
Deposit	10%	10,000
Legal fees		300
Survey fees		300
Refurbishment		2,000
	Total Investment	12,600
Mortgage amount		90,000
Rent per month	600	
Annual Rental		7,200
Mortgage interest @ 5%		-4,500
Insurance		-100
Repairs		-200
Service charge		
Agent fee		-846
	Annual profit	1,554
Return on investment (before tax)		12%

Example 1 with service charge		
Property Price		100,000
Deposit	10%	10,000
Legal fees		300
Survey fees		300
Refurbishment		2,000
	Total Investment	12,600
Mortgage amount		90,000
Rent per month	600	
Annual Rental		7,200
Mortgage interest @ 5%		-4,500
Insurance		-100
Repairs		-200
Service charge		-500
Agent fee		-846
	Annual profit	1,054
Return on investment (before tax)		8%

The service charge dramatically reduces the return and the cashflows generated.

There are ways to avoid the service charge but it involves getting the consent of everybody in the building - not a quick and easy task when the owner may not live there – and of course there is no guarantee that all owners will agree to ditch the existing service company and form their own management company.

Even if they do agree, somebody has to take on the running of the management company and chase for moneys owing. It is a thankless task.

My advice therefore is, **avoid flats and buy houses.** In fact, surveys show that terraced houses are the most favoured properties of buy to let investors.

Below is a summary of the main differences between buying a house or a flat:

HOUSES	
Advantages	**Disadvantages**
No service charge (which as already mentioned can be outrageously expensive)	More rooms to furnish if you provide a furnished let.
No tenants above or below (who may have leaking pipes, be noisy, or just overflow the bath)	Less secure, especially when empty.
Has a garden which can be an attraction to potential tenants	There is a garden to maintain during any void periods. Potential tenants are not attracted by an overgrown garden. There may be the problem of the tenants not maintaining the garden at all leading to an expense pf clearing it when they move out. Tenants may also sue the garden as a kind of dustbin where they throw anything from cigarettes to shopping trolleys.
May have a garage	A garage is another thing to maintain (roof, doors) and often collects rubbish.
Potentially more capital growth	More maintenance required – the whole building rather than a part needs to be maintained as well as external items (garden walls, garden...)
	Wiring, boilers, pipework etc are

	likely to be older and will need maintenance.
	Older houses are less energy efficient.
	Tenants may have children (which means lots of small repairs)

FLATS	
Advantages	**Disadvantages**
Less maintenance	Service charges
Shared costs of common areas such as corridors, roof, front door, entryphone	Less storage space.
Cheaper to buy	No garden
More secure to live in (entry phones)	Other tenants above and below may impact on the enjoyment of your property by their actions.
Usually near city centre so easy to let	Social housing can be an issue in new developments where a certain number of units are given to housing trusts. Sadly some housing trust tenants are not tidiest or quietest and you need to identify if they are located near any potential purchase.
	Oversupply in some areas. Check with a local estate agent what the situation in the area is. Sometimes developers have built the wrong kind of apartments (i.e. 2 bedroom apartments where the second bedroom is really an office and is too small to let in a flat share.

Key points from the chapter

- You can make more money from a similar priced house than a flat because of expensive service charges

CHAPTER 17

THINGS TO LOOK FOR WHEN BUYING

The important things is to find a property that needs as little work doing on it before you can rent it as possible. Work equals time equals loss of rent. Expect some minor items such as touching up paintwork.

Below are some basic things to look for:

Item	Detail
Location	The old saying of 'location location location' applies. Properties are more attractive to tenants if they are close to tube stations, bus stops, shops and restaurants (though not on top of shops and restaurants). A property located near a factory or industrial site or school will likewise be less attractive to potential tenants. Find out how far away the nearest bus stop is. You don't want it right outside the house because people waiting for a bus or getting off a bus can be noisy.
Property Condition	It goes without saying that the better the condition when bought the less work there is to do afterwards. Too many buyers focus on getting a reduction on the selling price by looking for defects than on finding a property without defects. Whilst you may legitimately find defects in the property that merit a price reduction you should divide them into 2 types – those that will need to be fixed before the property can be rented and those that are 'nice to have'. The difference is important because the survey result can affect the property valuation and therefore the amount that you can borrow. If you have to repair things you are effectively increasing the size of your deposit.

Items that are essential to check for are:

- damp

- cracks above door and on walls

- loose floor boards
- central heating and boiler – does it work, how old is the boiler and when was it last serviced, what type of fuel (gas is best), what type of pipes (plastic, copper, steel, lead), look for leaks
- wiring – look for old sockets, non-professionally installed sockets, old fuse box, burning on sockets
- kitchen condition – condition of units, are the worktops level, lighting, enough sockets,
- bathroom condition – condensation, mould, tilework, colour of fittings (avocado green) stained bowl, evidence of leaks, damp carpet, shower, smell, water pressure, condition of fittings, are they loose, flooring, does the water flow away quickly, how well does the toilet flush, is there a lock on the door, is the light pull cord broken
- ceilings and floors – sagging, cracks, loose floorboards
- windows – double glazing, condition of frames, do they open and shut correctly, and lock
- exterior – roof (inspect loft for evidence of leaks) look for missing tiles on outside, condition of walls and bowing, leaning chimneys,

Items that are nice to have are:

- flowers in the garden
- same colour carpet throughout
- a good view (but a bad view can be off putting)

Rentability

The property needs to be suitable for your target tenants. If you want to let to elderly people, steep stairs are not going to be attractive, but a flat with a lift would be. If you are looking to rent to students, they will each want a lock on the bedroom door and a large fridge (one shelf per student).

Neighbourhood

Have a look round the neighbourhood at different times of the day and night. It might seem obvious but not enough buy to let investors actually do this!

If schools are nearby and lots of children walk past the property observe how the children behave. Do they throw things into the gardens, run into the gardens, walk on the walls and generally behave well.

Make a visual inspection of neighbouring properties, cars, pubs, graffiti... What kind of neighbourhood is the property located in? Will tenants feel safe? Are the properties nearby empty or not?

One tip is to take plenty of pictures with a decent camera (at least 3 mega pixels) so you can review them later. Review them with somebody else who may spot things you didn't.

CHAPTER 18

THE PURCHASE PROCESS

Having made a decision to purchase a property there are several steps before you take possession. Several of these steps occur at the same time – the legal process runs the whole length while the mortgage offer and survey is happening.

Step 1:   Making an offer

Making an offer and getting the offer accepted is one of the most crucial parts of the buying process. If your offer is not accepted you will not be able to buy the property. It is therefore a good strategy to establish god relations with the estate agent. The game of offer and acceptance can take a while, or can be instant. Do your homework and see what other properties are selling for (you can check prices on the internet of the selling prices of other nearby properties) and see if there are any negotiating points on the property that can be used to reduce the selling price. Having the finance already in place can be a favourable thing if the seller wants to sell quickly. You are not going to be the link in the chain that will break. It is essential that you do the calculations to see what is the maximum price you are willing to pay. Do not pay more than this – there are millions of properties in the UK and there is no 'must have' property as a buy to let investor. Remember, it is not you who are going to live in the property as your home.

Step 2   Offer accepted

The agent will want to know the name of your solicitors, and how the property will be financed. They will also ask for evidence of your address and identity (original documents). The seller's estate agent will usually call you periodically to check how everything is going and to arrange the date and time when you will collect the keys.

Step 3   Obtaining the mortgage

Finding the finance is a key part of the purchase process and should be done as early as possible. You should prepare the last 6 months of payslips and bank statements (or last year's accounts if self-employed). The mortgage advisor will also ask for evidence of your address and identity (original documents). You should have an idea from a local letting agent of what the property is likely to rent out for.

There are hundreds of different types of mortgage deals out there, and an independent broker is the best bet.

Step 4   The legal process

The legal process is the most frustrating in my view. Lawyers in the UK rarely seem to understand the meaning of urgent. Overseas you can ask a question in the morning and receive a response or action in the afternoon. In the UK, one firm I berated for not acting quickly replied that they had acted within two weeks and they considered that quick! Be prepared for frustration therefore with your solicitor.

Given the above, try to find a solicitor from a personal recommendation. Note that even if you do manage to get the legal process done quickly the purchaser may not and the process gets delayed because of this. Usually the solicitor will ask for some money up front (£250 is not uncommon) plus the search fees. The solicitor will also ask for evidence of your address and identity (original documents)

What does the solicitor do? They will check that the seller has the right to sell the property (i.e. is the registered owner), they will send a questionnaire to the owner, and do the search at the local authority. The solicitor will send you an environmental report identifying such things as the location of telephone masts.

A contract is then prepared and you exchange. At this point you have to provide the deposit, usually 10% of the purchase price. (the deposit percentage can be negotiated)

Assuming the survey (see next) is accepted by the mortgage company, and that you have insurance (see below) you then complete. The mortgage company sends the balance to the solicitor (you, or your mortgage broker will need to chase them to make sure it arrives on the right day)

The solicitor will send you a completion statement – check it to make sure they have deducted the initial amount you paid.

Step 5   Survey

The local estate agent should be able to recommend a suitable firm of surveyors. The surveyors tend to be busy and booked in advance so you need to act quickly to avoid delays as the results of the survey affect the mortgage offer.

There are 3 types of survey:

1. valuation
2. homebuyers report
3. full survey

I recommend either the homebuyers report or the full survey, which give much more detail than a brief inspection. Typically, the surveys include a guide to repair costs which is useful.

Step 6   Insurance

You will need to provide details of buildings insurance to your solicitor before completion occurs. It is part of the mortgage requirement. Do shop around and don't necessarily take the cheapest quote. Check what the insurance covers, in particular what happens in void periods (length of period and how frequent the checks should be). Use the links section in Chapter 24 as a starting point for getting insurance quotes.

CHAPTER 19

BUYING AT AUCTION

As an investor you are always looking for value. As you will notice from the model spreadsheet one of the variables is the purchase price of the property. If you can buy below the market price you can increase your return. (In other words you are looking for a bargain). Auction prices are usually lower than the prices on the open market. There are many reasons for this – traditionally auctions have been used to dispose of property quickly

What to do before an auction

Read the catalogue

Go and see the property	Frequently the auctioneers/estate agents do blocking viewings at certain times only. They are usually on weekdays only. This can make it difficult to see all the properties you want to see if for example the viewing times are Tuesday 3 pm, Wednesday 10 am Thursday 2 pm. If you not live nearby it can be difficult to see the properties and if the viewings are not at a weekend it is impossible to see properties that are far away without taking time off work.
See what similar properties in the area sell for	This will give you some idea of what properties in good condition sell for and after making a reduction for the estimated cost of any refurbishment, how much you can borrow.
Check out the legal documents (may be a charge to get them, may have to visit)	The auctioneers usually have the legal documents relating to a property. You need to see these and understand them. Get copies for any properties you are intending to bid for. There may be a charge for supplying you with these.
Calculate maximum price	Stick to your maximum calculated price and do not exceed it.
Arrange a survey/valuation	takes time
Arrange a mortgage	Arranging a mortgage on an auction property is

	trickier than a normal purchase, partly due to the short timescales involved. You should be able to arrange at least the amount you can borrow subject to a satisfactory survey.
Get the addendum sheets	Not everything is always in the catalogue. There may be errors or omissions.
Check how to pay	Some auction houses accept credit cards, but most accept only debit cards or cheques. If you are not in the habit of carrying your cheque book around with you make sure you take it with you to the auction.
Be aware property may be withdrawn	If you are only bidding on one or two properties call the auction house just before the day of the auction to make sure the property is still in the auction.
Telephone bidding	If you cannot make the auction some auction houses will accept telephone bidding. You will have to provide a cleared cheque in advance for 10% of the guide price each property you are bidding on.

What to do during an auction

Obviously the bidding process is important and you need to make sure that the auctioneer sees you to identify that you have made a bid. It is a good idea to go to a previous auction to experience the sale so you are familiar with this on the day you want to make a bid.

Bring photographic ID and utility bill (originals only)

Bring a cheque book and/or a debit card

If you win you will have to pay an administration fee as well as the deposit.

What to do after an auction

There is a short period of time between the auction date and the date for paying the balance. This is usually 28 days. If you need to arrange a mortgage you will need a survey if you have not already had one and get the legal side moving as quickly as possible. It is therefore a good idea to have the mortgage lender and survey already prepared and choose a firm of solicitors that is used to dealing with the short deadlines from the auction process.

You should insure the property at once.

CHAPTER 20

THINGS TO DO ONCE YOU HAVE BOUGHT A PROPERTY

Once you have got the keys go and visit the property. It is a good idea to change the locks, particularly if the property has been rented out before. Go round the property with the lettings agent you are going to use and agree what needs to be fixed.

Remember that time is money and it is a good idea to have things arranged beforehand to avoid any delays. You will need a Corgi certificate for any gas appliances. Get the electrical system checked as well. Arrange this approximately two weeks before you take possession of the property. Likewise, if you know that the property will need some decoration of building work, arrange with a builder beforehand to come to the property as you take possession.

If you are managing the property yourself it is a good idea to already know the phone numbers of the local tradesman such as:

- Plumber

- Washing machine repairer

- Decorator

- Builder

- Corgi certified gas inspector (or use a nationwide company such as GAS-ELEC)

- The address and physical location of the local dump. (this can be hard to find in the phone book or council website being described as everything from refuse site to recycling centre!

- Local van hire company

- Cleaning company

- Carpet cleaning company

- Locksmith

- Gas supplier

- Electricity supplier
- Water company
- Local authority (for council tax)

Before letting you need to agree with your letting agent how you are going to manage the deposits of tenants. Since 6 April 2007 there is a mandatory scheme for managing deposits which gives the landlord two choices:

1. custodial, where the landlord must give the deposit to somebody else to administer

2. insurance based, which allows the landlord or the agent to retain the deposit monies.

Needless to say, most landlords will probably opt for the insurance based scheme.

CHAPTER 21

PROBLEMS

It is important for the investor to be aware that property investment does have it problems and does not always go smoothly. Before making starting out as a property investor it is important to consider the possible problems that can happen.

Problem	Details
Property is empty for a period of time	1. No rent comes in from tenants but the mortgage payments must still be made
	2. Need to check the wording of insurance policy for its validity during a period of unoccupancy. Some policies require a fortnightly check (which is not very convenient if you fare away)
	3. An empty property still incurs expenses – mortgage interest, insurance, council tax, utilities (the alarm needs electricity, workmen need electricity and/or water)
Tenants are behind with rent	Sadly this situation occurs more often than it should. It is essential to choose tenants wisely, and vet them before accepting them, both in terms of a credit reference, reference from previous or current landlord, and employment situation.
Tenants have stopped paying their rent	You need to talk to the tenants and find out why and how long this situation will last for. Ultimately you are going to have to go to court and evict them, which costs time and money. Given that it will take at least 2 months to evict the tenants and you have to pay legal

	fees, you might find it easier and cheaper to pay the tenants to leave immediately.
Tenants have damaged the property	The problem here is that you often discover this after the tenants have left. The deposit that they have given may not be enough to cover the repair bill.
Property needs repair	As a landlord with a short term let you are legally bound for repairs of certain items under the Landlord and Tenant Act 1985. These are:

- The structure and exterior of the dwelling

- Basins, sinks, baths and other sanitary installations

- Heating and hot water installations

Items in the property need to be repaired	Small repairs occur all the time, from small leaks in pipes to more extensive roof leaks.
	The most frequent items needing repairs are the boiler and the washing machine.
Tenants are (were) a couple and have split up.	You may be put in a difficult situation here in making a choice over who stays and who goes. Try to find out why they split up (such as unemployment) and choose the one with the best job. A single woman usually takes care of the property more than a recently girlfriendless male.
Tenants want more items in the property	Another difficult choice, but listen to what they need and what it costs. Balance the additional cost of what is being asked for against the cost of an empty property.

CHAPTER 22

CASE STUDY

By now you should have understood what kind of financial calculations you need to make before buying a property. Let's test them out using the situation described in the Daily Telegraph article. The article does not give us all the information so some assumptions will need to be made.

Information in the article	Assumed information
Cost of flat £125,000	85% mortgage of £106,250
	Interest only mortgage
	25 year term
	Deposit of £18,750
Flat needs new kitchen, bathroom, carpets and redecorating	Assumed costs are £5,000
	No service charge is mentioned so assumption is £200 per year.
	Agents fee of 10% plus VAT

With the above calculations we can produce a model of how the financial situation of the property might look like.

INTEREST ONLY MORTGAGE

Property Price		125,000
Deposit	10%	12,500
Legal fees		300
Survey fees		300
Refurbishment		5,000
Furniture		2,000
Total Investment		**20,100**
Mortgage amount		112,500
Rent per month	500	

Annual Rental	6,000
Mortgage interest @ 5%	-5,625
Insurance	-150
Repairs	-200
Agent fee	-705
Service charge	-200
Annual LOSS	**-880**

There is no tax to pay because the property makes a loss. The couple need to fund the property by £73 every month. After 25 years they will have funded £22,000. Whilst we may concede that property prices may well rise over the next 25 years, at the end of the mortgage period the couple will have to sell the property, repay the mortgage, pay capital gains tax and only then have money left over to pay themselves. Guessing what price the property might sell for in 25 years is pointless, because the couple will have been contributing each month over that period.

If the couple were buying with a repayment mortgage the situation is even worse from a cashflow point of view.

REPAYMENT MORTGAGE

Property Price		125,000
Deposit	10%	12,500
Legal fees		300
Survey fees		300
Refurbishment		5,000
Furniture		2,000
	Total Investment	**20,100**
Mortgage amount		112,500
Rent per month	500	
Annual Rental		6,000
Mortgage payments		-7,892
Insurance		-150
Repairs		-200
Agent fee		-705
Service charge		-200

Annual Cashflow   **-3,147**

Here the couple needs to fund the property by £262 every month or £78,675 over the term of the mortgage.

By now you will have realised why the strategy that the couple are pursuing is not their best strategy.

CHAPTER 23

SMALL COMPANY TIPS AND TRICKS

Below is a selection of things that can help you as a small company.

Fax number

You don't need to buy a fax machine! You can register with **efax** or **jfax** and **get a fax number for free**. The fax pops up on your email as a scanned document. If you need to scan a document and don't have a scanner, you fax the document to your own number and it arrives as a scanned document in your inbox!

www.efax.com

www.jfax.com

Stationery

Register your company with Staples to receive discounts on your stationery. The discounts are based on the quarterly spend.

www.staples.co.uk

Business Cards and Printing

Vistaprint will print your business cards for free, but the catch is that on the rear of the cards it advertises Vistaprint. All you pay for is the postage. Alternatively you can upgrade and pay for the cards and there is no advertising on the back. They have a wide variety of designs to choose from.

www.vistaprint.co.uk

Telephone calls for free

You will make a lot of phone calls as a property investor, so why not do it for free. You will need a computer and internet connection (broadband works best of course). **You can dial a UK landline for free with Cheapvoip.**

www.cheapvoip.com

www.skype.com

CHAPTER 24

LINKS ON THE WEB

I have included a selection of links that I have found useful. This is not a complete list by any means and you are welcome to send suggestions for inclusion in the next edition of the book, either of categories or the links.

Building Societies

Some building societies have specialised in the buy to let market and the first two below have been particularly helpful.

Note that for Birmingham Midshires their website says *"As a non advisory mortgage lender BM Solutions mortgage rates are only available through Independent Financial Advisers. For this reason, If you are a new customer you are required to contact your local IFA who will be able to advise you of the rates available to you. You can find a local Independent Financial Adviser by calling 0800 0853 250 or visiting www.unbiased.co.uk"*

Name	Telephone	Website
Portman	0845 845 7000	www.portman.co.uk
Birmingham Midshires	0845 300 2627	www.askbm.co.uk
Bristol and West	0117 979 2222	www.bristol-west.co.uk/
Northern Rock	0845 60 50 500	www.northernrock.co.uk

Mortgage Brokers

There is a huge range of brokers out there, almost one in every high street. I have used the first three listed and can vouch for their services. It is worth seeking out a specialist as there are many deals out there. It is likely that you will be offered a mortgage with a discounted rate for a number of years, and at the end of this period you may well wish to re-mortgage – a good relationship with a mortgage advisor is therefore essential.

Name	Telephone	Website
Alton Mortgages	0845 095 3435	www.altonmortgages.co.uk
John Charcol	0800 71 81 91	http://mortgages.charcolonline.co.uk

Name	Telephone	Website
The Money Centre	01603 428 500	www.themoneycentre.co.uk
Landlord Mortgages	0800 917 3324	www.lml.co.uk
Amicable	0800 781 0414	www.mortgagebestrate.co.uk
Paragon	0800 375777	www.paragon-mortgages.co.uk
Best 4 Let	0800 587 1008	www.best4let.com
ARLA		www.arla.co.uk/bt/lenders.htm

Limited Company Mortgages

There is a more restricted range of mortgage lenders for limited companies but the following have been helpful.

Note that many lenders will not lend to limited companies where the property value is less than £50,000, which can be a problem when buying terraced houses in the north of England.

Name	Telephone	Website
Alton Mortgages	0845 095 3435	www.altonmortgages.co.uk
Landlord Mortgages	0800 917 3324	www.lml.co.uk
First Union	0800 377 7653	www.firstunion.co.uk/
The Money Centre	01603 428 500	www.themoneycentre.co.uk
Mortgage Express	0500 111 130	www.mortgage-express.co.uk
Mortgages for Business	0845 345 6788	www.mortgagesforbusiness.com

Finding a property

You won't find all properties on the web, but Rightmove claims something like 85% of estate agents use them. It's as good a place to start as any other.

Name	Website
Rightmove	www.rightmove.co.uk
Find a property	www.findaproperty.com
Fish4Homes	www.fish4.co.uk/iad/homes
Prime location	www.promelocation.com

Auctions

Name		Website
Allsop	Nationwide	www.allsop.co.uk
Romans	Surrey and Hampshire	www.romans.co.uk/auctions_home.asp
Butters John Bee	Potteries	www.buttersjohnbee.com/
Pugh and Co	Northern England	www.roypugh.co.uk
Savills		www.savills.co.uk/
Harman Healy		www.harman-healy.co.uk/
Cushman and Wakefield		properties.cushmanwakefieldeurope.com/auction/

Property Insurance

Name	Telephone	Website
Endsleigh	0800 389 2011	www.endsleigh.co.uk/web/policies/landlord/index ml
Ashburnham Insurance Services	0800 169 6137	www.ashburnham-insurance.co.uk
Click4Quote. com	0845 089 9091	www.click4quote.com
Easy Let	0870 162 4885	www.easylet.org.uk

Accountancy, Tax, Legal, Company Formation and administration

Name	Telephone	Website
Landlord Law	01603 763 096	www.landlordlaw.co.uk
Tax café	01592 560 081	www.taxcafe.co.uk
MAAP accountants	01202 474545	www.maap.co.uk

Name	Telephone	Website
Company registrations online	0870 755 4545	www.companyregistrations.co.uk/guide-to-running-a-company.asp
Companies House	0870 333 3676	www.companieshouse.gov.uk/
TS Accounts	01473 407 314	www.tsaccounts.com
Taxation Solutions	0800 027 4533	www.propertytaxation.co.uk
Landlord Action	0870 765 2005	www.landlordaction.co.uk
Mills and Reeve	0870 600 0011	www.mills-reeve.com

Business Banking

Should you go the company route, the company will need a bank account. Unlike personal accounts there are many bank charges. The Abbey offers an account called Free Banking for Life (which has the limitation that you cannot pay in at the counter, only at the cashpoint machine) and Alliance and Leicester offered a good rate for deposit accounts for limited companies at the time of writing.

Name	Telephone	Website
Abbey National	0845 607 0666	www.anbusiness.com
Alliance and Leicester	0800 0565522	https://www.alliance-leicestercommercialbank.co.uk/content/HP000001.asp

Other

Name	Use	Website
Software	Software to enable you to keep track of your property portfolio	www.expertlandlord.com
Multimap	Online street map of the UK	www.multimap.co.uk
Streetmap	Online street map of the UK	www.streetmap.co.uk
Nationwide House price index	Find out how prices have moved historically	www.nationwide.co.uk/hpi/

Name	Use	Website
Yahoo! House Prices Centre	Check the prices of houses sold near to any post code	uk.houseprices.yahoo.net/
RLA	Residential Landlords Association	www.rla.org.uk/
Upmystreet	Find out everything about an area by typing in the postcode	www.upmystreet.com

APPENDIX A

TAX RATES FOR 2007/2008

Personal Allowance   5,225

Income Tax

Starting Rate 0-2,230   10%

Standard Rate 2,321-34,600   22%

Higher Rate 34,601-   40%

Capital Gains Tax

Annual Exempt Amount   9,200

For individuals, gains are reduced by taper relief reflecting the number of complete years after 5 April 1998.

The holding period required to receive maximum taper relief for business assets is two years, and for non-business assets is ten years

Years held after 5/4/98	Percentage of gain chargeable to CGT Business asset	Percentage of gain chargeable to CGT Non-Business asset
0	100%	100%
1	50%	100%
2	25%	100%
3	25%	95%
4	25%	90%
5	25%	85%
6	25%	80%

7	25%	75%
8	25%	70%
9	25%	65%
10	25%	60%

Stamp Duty

Property value 0-125,000	0%
125,001-250,000	1%
	(Note: 1% on total price, not just the amount above £125,000)
250,001-500,000	3%
Above 500,000	4%

VAT

VAT Threshold	64,000

Corporation Tax

Starting rate	20%

APPENDIX B

TAX RATES FOR 2006/2007

Personal Allowance   5,035

Income Tax

Starting Rate 0-2,150   10%

Standard Rate 2,151-33,300   22%

Higher Rate 33,301-   40%

Capital Gains Tax

Annual Exempt Amount   8,800

For individuals, gains are reduced by taper relief reflecting the number of complete years after 5 April 1998.

The holding period required to receive maximum taper relief for business assets is two years, and for non-business assets is ten years

Years held after 5/4/98	Percentage of gain chargeable to CGT Business asset	Percentage of gain chargeable to CGT Non-Business asset
0	100%	100%
1	50%	100%
2	25%	100%
3	25%	95%
4	25%	90%
5	25%	85%

6	25%	80%
7	25%	75%
8	25%	70%
9	25%	65%
10	25%	60%

Stamp Duty

Property value 0-125,000	0%
125,001-250,000	1%
250,001-500,000	3%
Above 500,000	4%

VAT

VAT Threshold	61,000

Corporation Tax

Starting rate	19%

Contact the author

Send any comments or suggestions to:

backtobackmodel@hotmail.co.uk

I am delighted to receive any feedback, whether about any errors you have discovered or any suggestions you have for improving the book in terms of content.

Please do also review the book on Amazon and Lulu.

www.amazon.co.uk

www.lulu.com/content/795526

www.ingramcontent.com/pod-product-compliance
Lightning Source LLC
Chambersburg PA
CBHW031948190326
41519CB00007B/718